Attorney & Law Firm

THE BUSINESS OF LAW

PLANNING & OPERATING FOR SURVIVAL & GROWTH

EDWARD POLL

GENERAL PRACTICE SECTION / AMERICAN BAR ASSOCIATION

Cover design by Jim Colao.

The material contained herein represents the opinions of the author and should not be construed to be the action of either the American Bar Association or the General Practice Section unless adopted pursuant to the Bylaws of the Association.

Nothing contained in this book is to be considered as the rendering of legal advice for specific cases, and readers are responsible for obtaining such advice from their own legal counsel. This book and any forms or agreements herein are intended for educational and informational purposes only.

© 1994 Edward Poll. All rights reserved.
Printed in the United States of America.

A major portion of this book has been reprinted from *Planning for a Successful Law Practice*, by Edward Poll. © 1994 Regents of the University of California. Reprinted with permission.

Library of Congress Catalog Card Number 93-72716
ISBN 0-89707-905-1

Discounts are available for books ordered in bulk. Special consideration is given to state bars, CLE programs, and other bar-related organizations. Inquire at Publications Planning & Marketing, American Bar Association, 750 North Lake Shore Drive, Chicago, Illinois 60611.

99 98 97 96   5 4 3 2

To my father, whose energy and enthusiasm for life's adventures seemed endless and whose love and compassion knew no boundaries . . . still my role model.

Contents

Preface ix
Acknowledgments xi
About the Author xiii

PART I: CREATING THE BUSINESS PLAN 1

CHAPTER 1 **Law Is a Business** 3
Law Is a Business 4
The Three Competencies 5
Warning Signs 7
Why Plan? 8

CHAPTER 2 **The Planning Process** 11
What Planning Is and Is Not 11
The Basic Steps 12
Who Plans? 14
The Logistics of Planning 15
Agreeing to Plan 15
Gathering the Relevant Information 16

CHAPTER 3 **Setting Goals** 21
Identifying Personal Goals 21
Identifying Law Firm Goals 22

CHAPTER 4 **Creating the Marketing Plan** 27
Components of a Marketing Plan 28
More Thoughts About Marketing 37

CHAPTER 5 **Creating the Financial Plan** 41
Key Financial Terms 42
Introduction to Cash Flow 44
Creating the Collected Revenue Cash Flow Form 45
Creating the Paid Expenses Cash Flow Form 50
Creating the SUMMARY Cash Flow Form 59
Congratulations! 64

Contents

CHAPTER 6	**Final Thoughts on Planning** 67
	Executing Your Plan for the First Time 67
	A Final Word About Planning 68
	Making It Work 68

PART II: TECHNIQUES FOR SURVIVAL AND GROWTH 69

CHAPTER 7	**Pricing Legal Services** 71
	Cost-Plus Pricing 71
	Market Pricing 73
	Cost Disbursements As an Element of Pricing 75
	Alternative Pricing Methods 75
	The Use of Non-Lawyers 79
	Price Sensitivity and Raising Rates 80

CHAPTER 8	**The Billing Process** 83
	Clients and the Billing Process 84
	Who Should Do the Billing? 84
	What Should Bills Look Like and Contain? 84
	When Should Bills Be Prepared? 85
	When Should Bills Be Sent? 88
	Responses From Clients 89

CHAPTER 9	**Credit and Collections** 91
	Giving Credit Where It Is Due 91
	Setting Your Credit Policy 92
	Collecting Your Money 93
	Steps to Increasing Your Collections 93

CHAPTER 10	**Methods of Determining Revenue** 99
	Revenue Pattern Analysis 99
	Turnover Ratio 100
	Aging Analysis 101
	Payment Pattern Analysis 103

CHAPTER 11	**Banks and Loans** 107
	Financial Needs 107
	What About a Loan? 109
	Types of Loans 110
	Selecting a Banker 110
	Getting to Know the Banker 112
	Understanding the Bank's Loan Requirements 113
	Documents the Bank Wants to See 114
	Additional Information to Discuss with the Bank 115

CHAPTER 12	**Should You Hire an Executive Director?** 117	

        The Executive Director's Job   117
        A Profit Center for the Firm   118
        Measuring Benefits   119

CHAPTER 13   **Playing the Slow Economy Game**   121
        Temporary Slowdown   121
        Downsizing   122
        Demerger   122
        Liquidation   123

CHAPTER 14   **Tricks of the Trade**   125
        Marketing   125
        Managing Your Finances   127
        Handling Clients   133
        Organizing Your Office   134

Glossary   137

APPENDIX A   **Cash Flow Projection Forms**   143

APPENDIX B   **Monthly Accounts Receivable Aging Analysis**   147

APPENDIX C   **Profit & Loss Statement**   151

APPENDIX D   **Budget Recap Revenue and Expense Forms**   153

APPENDIX E   **General Ledger Information**   157

APPENDIX F   **Payment Pattern Analysis**   161

Index   163

Preface

This book is the result of a lifelong attempt to combine my love for the law with my love for business.

In my early days, I was fortunate to observe and experience an entrepreneurial environment. My uncle was a shopkeeper, an owner of a neighborhood delicatessen in New York who retired to Los Angeles. He was bored with retirement and started another business, again a delicatessen. It grew, and he invited other members of the family—including my father—to join him in the enterprise. As the business expanded, it changed from a retail shop to a manufacturing business, making pickles and related condiments. As I was growing up, I learned to love the spirit and excitement of the business.

During this time, I was also observing another member of my family, who was one of the finest lawyers in the country and who believed in the highest principles of our profession. I looked upon him and his work with great admiration. It was with his influence and my observation that the law was a caring and helping profession that I decided to go to law school.

Throughout my career, I have always been involved in business ventures, even while practicing law. And I found that my law clients frequently asked for my advice in their business affairs while talking about their particular legal matters.

In the late 1980s, I was asked to manage a small but prestigious law firm in Beverly Hills. I realized then that management was the avenue that would permit me to combine my love of business with my love of law. I wanted to help colleagues in the legal profession improve the way they help *their* clients.

At about the same time, I talked to friends who were involved with risk-management companies, malpractice insurance carriers, and the State Bar of California. They startled me with the statistics of disciplinary proceedings before the Bar and of malpractice complaints. I learned that at least half of all consumer complaints were caused by poor management practices of lawyers! If I could reach out to my colleagues in the profession with my knowledge of business, then I could make a contribution. Thus, I started a new career: law practice management consultant.

I was fortunate enough to work with Willis S. Baughman, Vice President of Loss Prevention, Lawyers Mutual Insurance Company of California. LMIC sponsored practice management programs throughout the State. As part of these programs, I talked to the insureds of LMIC about the financial management of their practices. Many of my ideas were refined as a result of these discussions and presentations.

I also had the good fortune to be invited to speak to the profession throughout the country. People I have known for years in the General Practice Section of the American Bar Association made it possible for me to learn about the needs of lawyers all over the United States.

All of this, however, brings me back to a basic tenet that I learned while working with my father in the manufacturing business many years ago. And that is that the *client* (or customer) must *feel taken care of* and must feel that he or she is receiving good quality service for the money being paid. It does not matter whether the product is a 5-cent pickle from a barrel or legal services at $250 per hour. The client or customer is king, and *their perception* of the quality and value of the service is paramount. Lawyers need to look up from the form books, the treatises, the cases, and the statute books to find out who their clients really are and what they expect. If I can help lawyers understand this process and help them improve their office and financial procedures so that they can provide caring, understanding, and effective legal services to clients, my objective will have been achieved.

This book, then, is designed to help you—attorneys and law firms, start-ups, solos, and small-firm practitioners, fee-based and contingency lawyers—accept the twin principles of planning for the future and running your practices as businesses.

My primary goal is to describe a plan of action that is workable and manageable and that you will use and refer to frequently. Part I describes the how and why of creating a business plan; Part II gives additional strategies and techniques to implement when carrying out the business plan.

After reading the book, I hope you will have—or be ready to prepare—a completed plan consisting of three components (goals, marketing, and finances) with one to three pages in each section. That is right—only one to three pages each. That is a total of less than ten pages. But those ten pages will probably be the most important you will ever prepare. They will represent what your practice is all about and where you're going with it.

This work comes out of my love of the profession and my hope that I can help make your practice more profitable and more effective in the delivery of quality legal services for your clients. I welcome any comments and suggestions that you may have.

Edward Poll, J.D., M.B.A.
421 Howland Canal
Venice, California 90291
TEL: (310) 827-5415
FAX: (310) 578-1769

Acknowledgments

No venture can be completed by one person alone. The expression that "no man is an island" is very literally true in today's modern environment. We all depend on one another for a whole host of things we use in our daily life and we frequently take them for granted.

As dependent as we may be, however, one does not fully realize that dependence until we either are faced with a crisis or undertake a project of special significance to us. In my case, I developed a strong desire, almost a need, to produce this book. I began it not really knowing the full ramifications of the time and commitment that would be required. I had written other materials, even a chapter in a book. But this is my first complete book, not just a chapter or monograph. There is a difference.

I can never express fully my appreciation and gratitude to the many people who, over the years, contributed to my growth, my learning, and my experience. This, particularly, includes my wife, Paula, and our children, all of whom are well along the path of success in their respective fields of endeavor. To those whose paths I crossed on the road to my being where I am today, I thank you. I value your contribution and friendship, and I hope to visit with you again.

For those who were directly involved in the process of writing and preparing this book, I also say thank you. Colleagues in the Bar, and particularly the General Practice Section of the American Bar Association and the General and Solo Practice Section of The State Bar of California, were and continue to be more than generous in their encouragement and support of my dreams. Continuing Education of the Bar (C.E.B.), University of California, made suggestions for improvement in my concepts and, in the process, forced me to clarify my thoughts. And, in particular, I want to thank Suzanne E. Graber, Department Manager, Action Products, for her continuing faith that I could complete what I said I would do and for her guidance when I didn't quite understand the world of publishing and its requirements.

I want to thank Harald Johnson, president of Crawford Communications, for his support and contributions. Without his help in the writing of this book, the project would still be on the table, waiting for one more chapter. But, more importantly, he was the first person I turned to when I embarked on my new career as a law firm management consultant several years ago. Upon leaving

Acknowledgments

the active practice of law after more than twenty years, I developed my marketing approach with Harald and we have worked together ever since.

Lastly, I'd like to thank Julie Viereck, my assistant. She has taken many tasks from me, performed them ably, and thereby allowed me the time to work toward fulfilling this dream.

With this team intact, I look forward to continuing the journey forward.

About the Author

Edward Poll, J.D., M.B.A., is a law firm management consultant, educator, and lawyer in Los Angeles, California. He consults with lawyers and law firms, leads seminars on the business of law practice, and lectures before bar associations and other law groups on the subject of cash flow and law practice management. Mr. Poll has been an instructor for the Institute of Continuing Legal Education (ICLE) at the University of Michigan, Ann Arbor, Michigan. Mr. Poll has also taught "Creating New Business Enterprises" in the Department of Entrepreneurship, University of Southern California School of Business; "Business of Law Practice" in the Advanced Professional Education program at the Law Center of the University of Southern California (USC); and "Starting Your Own Business" at the University of California, Los Angeles (UCLA). Mr. Poll is also the creator and instructor of a new course at UCLA designed to teach the skills of law firm administration.

Mr. Poll has published numerous articles on law practice management and has been a frequent contributor to legal and business publications, including *The Compleat Lawyer, Law Practice Management, California Lawyer, Los Angeles Lawyer, The Practical Lawyer, Law Office Economics & Management, Lawyers Weekly USA,* and *California Law Business* (supplement to the Los Angeles Daily Journal).

Mr. Poll has the unique blend of twenty-five years of law practice (including civil litigation and corporate/business law) and business experience (CEO, COO, and Managing Attorney).

PART I
Creating the Business Plan

CHAPTER I
Law Is a Business

Law is an honorable profession, but it is also a business. The two concepts are the yin and yang for the delivery of quality legal services.

[author unknown]

Chapter Checklist   **Law Is a Business**
The Three Competencies
Warning Signs
Why Plan?

Brad Waters was really upset. He had just received the notice from the state bar. A doctor involved in a case that was settled had filed a complaint with the bar, claiming that Waters had not sent him his check. Yes, it was true, but he was going to as soon as he could get around to it. He was busy.

Very busy. He was the sole lawyer in his seven-person private practice. Here he was with very large gross revenues each year from his small law firm, but he just did not seem to have enough time. And he could never figure out where the money was, nor did his accounts receivable ever seem to get smaller.

"Why," he thought, "am I getting so bogged down? I just want to do what I do best—practice law."

Although the name is fictitious, the scenario is not. Waters's complaint from the doctor is merely the symptom of a much larger problem. In the past fifteen years, there has been an explosion in lawyer discipline complaints. In California, this increase mirrors the surge in the number of the state's lawyers (approximately 150,000 as of this writing). In fact, 75 percent of the State Bar of California's annual budget is allocated to its lawyer discipline system. And in 1991, that state's bar received 76,858 complaints, investigated 6,447 of them, and prosecuted 1,345 cases.

By far, the most common complaints (39 percent) concerned lawyers' performance, mostly failure to perform, delay, abandonment, or failure to communicate. And one of the main reasons that small firms or sole practitioners get into trouble—with their

Part I: *Creating the Business Plan*

state bar or with their own cash flow—is due to an inability or unwillingness to run the *business* of the practice efficiently.

Let's admit it: Most lawyers (and I am one of them) are egocentric. They require that the control of a matter remain in their hands. "Client control" is a favorite phrase among lawyers. Therefore, they believe that they know how to run their offices. But when faced with the fact that lawyers are all busy taking care of their primary task—advocating their clients' interests—it becomes clear that the management of a law practice takes a secondary position. And if lawyers are not able to take care of their own business, they obviously are not going to do a very good job of taking care of their clients. And that attitude leads to trouble.

During my more than twenty years of law practice, I have observed that a few lawyers and law firms are acutely conscious of the business aspects of running a practice. They deliver legal services with a view to the costs and benefits of those services. That is, they try to balance the benefits to be achieved with the cost of delivering those benefits.

But, unfortunately, most do not. Some, like the lawyer in our example above, are frequently overworked, underorganized, and lacking in the basic business skills to make their practices run more efficiently. Are these lawyers delivering "quality" legal services?

Successful law firms pay attention to the needs and desires of their clients. Successful law firms are able to communicate this awareness of and sensitivity to the client's wishes to the client. Successful law firms deliver their services at a price that does not offend the client. And finally, successful law firms know how to run the *business* of their practice.

LAW IS A BUSINESS

Most lawyers would now agree—although some grudgingly—that "law is a business." This recognition indicates a dramatic change from recent times. Today, most acknowledge that law is a professional service business and that there is a need to pay attention to business factors previously ignored or given little public expression. Factors like marketing, collection of accounts receivable, write-offs, cash flow, leverage and others that hint at attempts to understand the business and make the business more efficient and profitable are beginning to be popular topics of study among lawyers today. Yes—law is an honorable *profession*, but it is also a *business*. The two concepts are the yin and yang (complementary halves) of the delivery of quality legal services.

Most professionals have not been prepared to deal with the recent economic downturn. Lawyers witnessed or experienced the "go-go" days of the 1980s, which saw the gigantic explosion of regional firms into meganational law firms with hundreds of lawyers. There were rumors of huge partner draws. Almost everyone painted pictures that were rosier and rosier. Yet, during that heady time, most firms were not addressing certain basic economic issues. And those moments of inattention inevitably led to trouble.

Feeling the new economic pressures, law firms that failed to have sound basic economic policies in place began to crumble. Some lawyers had come to believe that it was their inalienable right to increase their own personal economic well-being each year. But other factors emerged that began to thwart that belief. Some realized that they were not able to collect what was owed to them because of their clients' economic woes; or they could not get new clients; or they found it tougher to compete, with an increasing number of lawyers fighting for a decreasing number of solvent clients/customers. Then came the highly publicized break-ups or "de-mergers" of several major national firms, such as Finley, Kumble, et al. The economic turmoil that has been facing the legal profession is being felt by all lawyers, not just the big firms. All lawyers are asking serious questions about the economics of their practices—questions like: "How can we collect our accounts receivable?" "Should we hire an outside executive director to manage the practice?" "How do we attract more and better clients?" and "How can I better manage my practice?"

These are all legitimate "business" questions, but before lawyers can begin to answer them, they need to understand how businesses—including law practices—function.

THE THREE COMPETENCIES

All businesses—whether they are law firms, pickle factories, sheet metal fabricators, or swimming pool cleaning services—have to do three things to survive and grow:

- Get customers.
- Do quality work.
- Get paid.

If you fall down in any of the three areas, you will ultimately fail. You can package the best-tasting pickles in the world, but if you cannot find enough customers, or those customers do not pay you on time, you will soon be out of business.

It is no different in the legal field. Getting—and keeping—customers is called marketing or practice development. Doing the work is the substantive work of lawyering, and getting paid is the financial part, and some would say the best part.

Here, then, is the basic structure of a legal business in terms of competencies:

Part I: *Creating the Business Plan*

> The Three Competencies: Marketing (get the customer)
> Technical (do quality work)
> Financial (get paid)

Marketing Competence

As recently as the 1970s, law schools gave little or no instruction in marketing competence, or getting—and keeping—the customer. Aside from a course or two in "client relations," not much was done about marketing. In the 1980s, law schools started to put more effort into this area, but not until the beginning of the 1990s did we begin to see a serious effort, at least at the practitioners' level, given to marketing. Law schools, generally, have still not yet addressed this issue appropriately.

But such marketing concepts as pricing and differentiation have now become critical to the survival of firms, and we will discuss them at length later in this book.

Technical Competence

In the 1960s and 1970s, the *only* issue of concern to the profession was technical competence, or as I like to call it, doing quality legal work. Law schools structured their curricula to provide students with the greatest amount of knowledge in substantive law. It used to be that lawyers thought only about "lawyering," or doing a good job for the client—creating an estate plan, putting a brief together, arguing a case, etc. But now we need to expand our definition of technical competence.

Today, we know that "doing a good job" includes SERVICE, and that service includes new concepts (or old concepts merely renamed), such as improved client relations, "bonding," quality, etc. Successful lawyers have been attuned to the idea of service from the beginning, but for many others this is new ground. While substantive law is outside the scope of this book, some of the client relations aspects of a law practice are appropriate for our discussion because they impact the other two areas: marketing and finance. More about these later.

Financial Competence

Currently, issues concerning financial competence are beginning to appear in the legal press. Undoubtedly, the most apparent reason for this is that the economic pressures clients have experienced during the last several years (dating at least from the "Crash of '87") are, finally, being passed on to professionals such as lawyers and accountants.

Financial competence is, of course, more than collecting your fees or your contingency recovery. Financial competence is the ability to manage the affairs of the law firm relating to money, either personally or through designated persons. In the end, being financially competent means that you are able to make and keep more money than you spend!

Marketing and finance are two of the most critical—yet to most lawyers, mysterious—elements in determining whether a law practice will succeed in today's tough economic climate. They are the basis for our discussion about law as a business and planning for success.

WARNING SIGNS

Since professional service businesses must now face the test of the market along with everyone else—due to more competition for fewer and more-sophisticated clients (consumers of legal services), recessionary forces, and a maturing market, among other factors—it is important to analyze specific planning strategies in the context of the business of the law.

Most lawyers begin to realize that they are in trouble only when the money ceases to come in the door. However, cash flow cessation is usually the *last* symptom of a downward spiral that started long before.

Here are some basic indicators that may signal that the business of your practice needs some first aid:

- Deteriorating firm financial performance
- Lower partner draws (taking less money home)
- Poor firm cash flow, i.e., not enough money coming in compared to money going out
- Clients taking longer to pay (aging accounts receivable)
- Fewer clients (especially fewer healthy clients)
- More noticeable competition for new clients
- Working more hours but feeling as if you are falling behind
- Shrinking practice areas
- Increases in client complaints
- Lack of trust among partners
- Compensation, management structures, and management teams that change every few years
- Poor morale among associates and staff
- High turnover among lawyers

Look at an example of warning signs from the world of sports. Your law practice is like an athlete who is exercising in hot weather. Hydration—maintaining adequate body fluids—is critical to an athlete's performance and even his health. In fact, *dehydration* (losing water) can lead to serious medical problems like heat exhaustion, heat stroke, and ultimately death.

In hot weather, when athletes are competing vigorously for extended periods, it is common for water loss to exceed water intake. As dehydration sets in, the body diminishes its sweat rate to conserve remaining water supplies. When this happens, the body starts to overheat because sweating is how the body cools itself.

Unfortunately, the body's ability to detect dehydration is slow. When you first begin to feel thirsty, your body weight has already decreased 0.5 to 2.0 percent from loss of fluids. In other words, there is a lag time between when the body is starting to become dehydrated and when it sends a signal (thirst) for you to head to the nearest water fountain to do something about it. Knowledgeable athletes anticipate this problem by drinking plenty of fluids *before* and *during* exercise, even if they are not thirsty.

A law practice works the same way. The point when the cash has stopped coming in the door is much too late to start wondering if you may have a problem. You do. The seeds of the problem were undoubtedly sown weeks, months, or even years earlier.

Like our overheated athlete, you need to think about your practice's business *before* you run into problems. This is usually called planning ahead, and the point of this book is to help you plan *now* so you will not find yourself in the middle of the race without a drinking fountain in sight.

WHY PLAN?

Driving from Los Angeles to Chicago requires a plan. You could just take off in a northeasterly direction from L.A. and hope for the best, but a better strategy is to open up a road map of the United States and plot the best route to get you to your destination. The map, along with your objectives (scenic versus shortest route), and your program for stopping to sleep, eat, and refuel, all comprise your plan.

A scene from Lewis Carroll's *Alice's Adventures in Wonderland* is another good analogy. Alice, trying to find her way, encounters the Cheshire Cat sitting in a tree, and asks:

"Would you tell me, please, which way I ought to walk from here?"

"That depends a good deal on where you want to get to," said the Cat.

"I don't much care where," said Alice.

"Then it doesn't matter which way you walk," said the Cat.

"So long as I get *somewhere*," Alice added as an explanation.

"Oh, you're sure to do that," said the Cat, "if you only walk long enough."

In today's economy, walking long enough to get to an undefined destination is a recipe for disaster. The path to nowhere in particular is the path to failure.

In addition to consulting with law firms, I also teach regular business and entrepreneur classes. One difference I have noticed between the two groups (lawyers and business students) is that, in general, the lawyers are leery of planning, while the business students of today accept planning for the future as a natural and necessary topic of discussion. Why do lawyers seem to have so much trouble accepting the concept of business planning? There are four main objections, or "excuses."

First, believing that the law is "an honorable profession," lawyers somehow think that attention to the business side of the practice is demeaning or "unprofessional." Worrying about the money is somehow considered beneath them, a necessary evil that would best be left to its own natural actions or to private thoughts. But an open discussion or, heaven forbid, actual planning for the firm's success—now that is giving the subject way too much visibility and importance. How crass. How dishonorable. Sound familiar?

Second, lawyers feel they do not have the training to handle business decisions. And many just do not want to. After all, if they had wanted to learn about business, they would have gone to business school, not law school, right? Although law is a caring, helping profession, and lawyers are generally quick learners, most lawyers already spend so much energy, time, and effort learning the substantive areas of their practice that they have little or no time or desire to learn business skills.

Third, planning is complex, intimidating, and just plain boring. There probably is not one of you who is reading this book who has not thrown up your hands in disgust and had your eyes glaze over after trying to muddle through a complex business-plan format, a cash-flow textbook, or a planning treatise. This stuff is basically horrible torture, is it not?

Fourth, there just is not enough time to spend on nonlegal matters these days. Everyone seems to be working ten-, twelve-, or fourteen-hour days as it is. How can anyone squeeze any more time out of the day?

Let's counter these criticisms directly. First, "business" is not dishonorable at all. Doctors do it, architects do it, every successful person does it. In fact, and as stated before, law *is* a business. Anyone who does not understand that is living in the past. Second, with regard to training, any reasonably intelligent lawyer can learn the basics of planning and business without having to get bogged down by the details. Third, while it is true that traditional studies on this subject have been anything but user-friendly, it does not have to be so, and one of my goals is to make all this gibberish SIMPLE and UNDERSTANDABLE. Fourth, and I know this may sound threatening, you had better find some time to think about the business of your practice, or time may be all you will have left!

The world has changed, and the practice of law has changed right along with it. Make no mistake about it—the "stick-your-business-head-in-the-sand" approach to the practice of law is dead, if it *ever* existed. Lawyers who have been slow to accept this concept of business planning are now paying the price. The old way of a firm just rolling along at the whims of its strongest partners—without a cohesive vision or plan that binds all the partners, associates, and staff—is obsolete. In our current treacherous economic waters, if all the crew are not rowing in the same direction, the boat is very likely to sink!

No matter how you measure your success, whether it be in business terms, personal terms, or both, a failure to plan is a plan to fail.

The future is not a result of choices among alternative paths offered by the present, but a place that is created—created first in the mind and will, and created next in activity. The future is not someplace you are going to but one you are creating. The paths to it are not found, but made.

The opportunity for utilizing the primary tool of good management—effective business planning—is here and available. The purpose of this book is to guide you in that planning process. The question is, What do you plan to do about planning for your success?

CHAPTER 2
The Planning Process

For everything, you must have a plan.

—Napoleon

Chapter Checklist
What Planning Is and Is Not
The Basic Steps
Who Plans?
The Logistics of Planning
Agreeing to Plan
Gathering Relevant Information
Action Plan

WHAT PLANNING IS AND IS NOT

A plan is a scheme or program for making or doing something; it is a detailed method, formulated beforehand, of proceeding on a course of action.

Since what we are discussing here is the *business* of the practice of law, our plan is appropriately called a business plan.

A good business plan:

- Is simple to understand
- Requires effort and time to create
- Is ongoing and evolving, being changed as circumstances change and more accurate information is gathered
- Is based on shared beliefs
- Is agreeable to and supported by all those with responsibility to act—staff as well as lawyers

A bad business plan:

- Is overly complex and intimidating
- Is academic, without practical applications
- Is "carved in stone" and inflexible
- Has limited support

Business planning is an idea and an action that can be accomplished regardless of the nature of the substantive area of your

Part I: Creating the Business Plan

practice. This process applies to transactional work (usually based on hourly billing, fixed/flat fee, etc.) and to contingency practice such as personal injury or to debt collection (usually based on a percentage of the fee recovered without reference to the time invested by the lawyer).

Contrary to what many people think, a business plan does not need to be a thick document with a fancy binder. The problem with most business plans is that they are too complicated and too intimidating. Consequently, they are typically and quickly put on a shelf, never to see the light of day again. A plan that is not used is no plan at all.

The most difficult part of creating any plan is getting started. What information is required? How do you proceed? What are the steps to take? It is common for there to be a certain amount of fear associated with this kind of "big-picture" planning, and lawyers are not immune to feeling it.

You do not need to feel frightened about business planning, however, even if you have never done it before. As mentioned in the previous chapter, planning should first and foremost be SIMPLE and UNDERSTANDABLE. It should also be LOGICAL.

THE BASIC STEPS

Rather than being afraid of planning, lawyers should actually feel confident, since they are trained to think logically about problems and solutions. Planning is merely one form of problem solving. And like all problem solving, the business planning process has certain steps. Although there are plenty of twelve- and fifteen-step planning processes out there, I believe they are too complicated or abstract for the average lawyer to put into practice. My goal is to simplify the process of running a successful law practice to its essential elements. Here are the basic steps in business planning that we will be using:

POLL'S BASIC BUSINESS PLANNING STEPS

- Prepare to plan (agree to plan and gather information).
- Identify your goals.
- Create the marketing plan.
- Create the financial plan.
- Evaluate and compare the results with your goals and revise the plan(s) if necessary.

Let's take a brief look at each of these steps.

Prepare to Plan

In a law firm, it is important for all the key players to agree on the direction of the firm. If the partners are not clear about the overall goals as well as specific objectives and strategies, then the

Chapter 2: The Planning Process

planning process is bound to be sabotaged and ineffectual. Partners need to "buy in" to a plan. Solos are not immune from this requirement either. They must get a spouse or "significant other" to accept the general direction of the firm. That is why the first element of any plan is to agree to make and abide by the plan.

You need to gather a certain amount of historical information so that you can analyze it and start thinking about realistic modifications for the future. Plans for the future need not mandate growth; in a stagnating economy, planning to stay at the present level of revenue or size may be the most that a lawyer can expect. You will be primarily interested in marketing and financial data in the form of documents, statistics, reports, survey results, and, when there is nothing else, your best guesses. All this data will give you a snapshot of you or your firm's marketing and economic health *in the present*. Once you can see where you have been, it is much easier to see where you can go. We will talk about the specific marketing and financial information you will need in the next chapter.

Identify Goals

If you do not decide what type of practice you want, you will wind up with one reflecting whatever walks in the door. Serendipity or whim may make you successful, but it is doubtful. You need to decide what you want to be and what you want to do, both professionally and personally. Remember Alice and the Cheshire Cat. We will go into more detail about goals in chapter 3.

Create the Marketing Plan

Since your practice is dependent on customers, or clients, then getting them and keeping them is obviously critical to your success. A marketing plan helps you to see who these elusive people are and how to attract them to your door. Marketing is absolutely crucial to any business, and law practices are not exempt. We will discuss marketing at length in chapter 4.

Create the Financial Plan

The financial plan is the culmination of all your earlier information gathering, thinking, and planning. The financial plan is the statement, in financial or monetary terms (the language of business), of your dreams and goals. We will go into more detail about the financial plan in chapter 5.

Evaluate and Revise the Plan

Good planning is not static; it is meant to be a guide that you can judge actions or outcomes against. If you begin to notice that a certain aspect of a plan is not working or needs some adjustment,

Part I: Creating the Business Plan

change it. The beauty of a flexible plan is that it can be revised to better reflect the reality of your specific situation and to help you get to your desired outcome. Planning is an ongoing process.

I call these five steps taken together a business plan, and the emphasis is clearly on the three that are the most important: setting GOALS, creating a MARKETING PLAN, and creating a FINANCIAL PLAN. We are going to spend more time concentrating on these elements or steps because they hold the key to your practice's business success. Another way of saying it is this: You need to decide where you are going and what you want to be (goals), you need to set into motion marketing actions to get you there (marketing plan), and you need to manage the financial resources to make it all happen (financial plan).

WHO PLANS?

Business planning in a law firm requires a commitment from *all* the key individuals. Who should be involved in the planning process is an important question. If you are a solo practitioner, the answer is easy: you are the planner. But the solo who has no other staff also has the disadvantage of having no one else to talk to or to bounce ideas off. In that case, solos should consider involving a spouse or significant other, or consider accountants, bankers, or even outside law firm management consultants, as long as they have some understanding of the legal field and you trust their judgment.

In small firms with more than one lawyer, *all* lawyers, whether partners or associates, should be invited to participate in planning. If not, someone who is not a part of the process can, and probably will, attack the outcome.

What about including staff? Opinions are split on this question. Reasons to include staff in the planning process include: They have a better idea of the practical, day-to-day activities of the office; they will be more motivated if they have input into the planning; and it is proof that you value their contributions and that you think they are worthy of your trust.

Reasons *not* to include staff include: lawyers may feel inhibited about "telling it like it is"; the staff will have access to confidential information; staff should not be involved in the overall direction of the firm.

The best choice is to include your staff in the planning process. Everyone wants to feel that they are part of the team. And when they feel part of the team, they usually act more responsibly if they had some input into the process. Staff, especially in a small firm, have knowledge and insight into the firm that owners or partners frequently do not. An administrator or manager, if there is one, is a good example of a staff member who should be involved in the planning process. Administrators usually have a

Chapter 2: The Planning Process

unique perspective and significant practical information about the firm.

Also, when staff members understand the goals of the firm, they may be more inclined to help generate revenue through *their* own network of contacts.

Two people on a tandem bicycle can go faster than one person alone, so try to include other "riders" on the planning vehicle.

THE LOGISTICS OF PLANNING

What about confidentiality? Although full disclosure is the best way to discuss the direction of the firm accurately, firm owners are sometimes reluctant to open up financial information like gross receipts, expenses, salaries, or draws with associates or staff. One solution is to convert all the sensitive facts to percentages or averages.

Where do you plan? For the small firm, a series of meetings or maybe a weekend retreat are the best options. In either case, it is important to get away from the daily interruptions of the office. In fact, it sometimes helps to get as far away as possible. Most of you know the feeling of being able to see your business in a different perspective when you are away from it.

If you cannot go away on a retreat-type weekend, consider a conference room with *no* telephone or office interruptions. A planning meeting requires complete focus.

How do you run a planning meeting? Other than the principals, there are two specific people needed: a facilitator and a reporter. The facilitator's job is to encourage and assist the flow of communications. Consequently, the facilitator should *not* be the strongest partner or the most dominant person in the firm, otherwise he or she will impose his or her opinions on rest of the group. The rest of the group might as well go home; the meeting will be a waste of time.

The reporter documents all the discussions and decisions so that no one forgets what was accomplished.

The main point about the actual meeting or meetings is that they should be nonthreatening; no one should dominate. The purpose is to come to a consensus that includes everyone's input. Strong partners need to step back to allow others the chance to articulate their contributions. The whole group should understand and practice a nonjudgmental policy; no put-downs, no ridicule is allowable if open communication is to be encouraged.

AGREEING TO PLAN

All the partners need to "buy into" the planning process. If some are lukewarm to the idea, you need to do your best to "sell" the planning idea to all concerned. Provide key decision makers with planning articles and books, planning documents, white papers, and other reports on industry and professional trends and forecasts. Maintain a constant stream of planning information and materials. Someone—and it might have to be you—may need to promote the importance of planning to the firm. It may be in *your* best interest.

GATHERING THE RELEVANT INFORMATION

Now is the time to gather the appropriate historical information about the firm that will serve as the starting point for discussing the future. This information will be concerned with both marketing and financial issues, and will come from both inside and outside the firm. We will discuss the future in much more detail in chapters 4 and 5.

In the meantime, try to gather as much of the following types of information as possible.

Firm Financial Information

- Financial statements of the law practice for the last five years, or less if you are a new practitioner. These statements are normally prepared by the firm's bookkeeper or accountant. They usually consist of documents entitled balance sheet, income statement, and, possibly, cash or cash flow statements (more about these later);
- Tax returns of the law practice for the last five years (if available). These may be your Schedule C, the law partnership tax return, or the professional law corporation tax return;
- Aging of accounts receivable, if any;
- Billing records, including ledger cards showing billings and payments over time by individual clients;
- A checkbook register showing all checks written, the name of the payee, and the amount and type of expense;
- Previous plans or projections prepared by or for you;
- Bank statements for your general account;
- Bank statements for your clients' trust accounts.

General Marketing Information

- Articles/statistics about legal marketing trends;
- Law firm surveys from bar groups;
- Basic demographic information about your *current* client base, showing number of clients, types of business, scope of services, legal requirements, etc.;
- Basic demographic information about your *prospective* clients, such as industry, size, and type of services required.

Chapter 2: The Planning Process

You are encouraged to add to the above by gathering additional economic information that will help you fill in the gaps in picturing your firm. How many people were employed at your firm at the end of last year? Break it down by partners, associates, of counsel, etc. How many contingency versus fee-based lawyers? What is the average hourly rate for partners/shareholders? For associates? What was the annual average number of billable hours for the same groups for last year? Chances are, your accountant or bookkeeper will not be able to answer questions such as these. So to acquire valuable information of this type, you will need to do a simple survey. Use the Law Firm Economic Survey form (see Figure 2.1 on pages 18 and 19), copy it, and encourage lawyers and staff to fill it out as honestly and completely as possible. Add to the questions or change them if you like, but get this kind of information! The more information you have, the easier it will be for you to see weaknesses, strengths, and areas for improvement at your firm.

While you are gathering all this information, keep a portion of your attention open to the future. If you see obvious problem areas or areas of opportunity, jot them down. In fact, make up a sheet, call it something like "Changes/Needs/Opportunities" and jot down any fact or observation that strikes you as important. This will ensure that you will not forget important ideas or "flashes of enlightenment." You will be able to pull them out for discussion at the appropriate point later.

ACTION PLAN

- Get the agreement and commitment to start the planning process.
- Schedule the planning meetings.
- Gather relevant information and fill out the Law Firm Economic Survey.

FIGURE 2.1   **Law Firm Economic Survey**

BUSINESS STRUCTURE

1. How many of the following were employed at your firm as of December 31, 199X? *(fill in number of all that apply)*

- Partners/shareholders..............
- Associate lawyers ....
- Of counsel ....
- Paralegal ....
- Secretaries ....
- Administrative staff ....

2. Your firm's business structure is a: *(check only one)*

- Professional corporation ....
- Partnership........................
- Sole proprietorship.................

3. Do you have a: *(check all that apply)*

- Managing partner/shareholder ....
- Management committee ....
  - Number of members ....
- Nonlawyer chief executive officer .....
- Full-time executive director ....
- Part-time executive director ....

4. Does your firm have a partnership or shareholder agreement?
    Yes ☐   No ☐
  Is it: Written? ☐   Oral? ☐

FINANCIAL INFORMATION

5. 199X Annual Gross billings ..... $ _____
6. 199X Annual Gross receipts .... $ _____
7. 199X Annual Expenses: *(estimate where needed)*

  EMPLOYEE SALARIES
- Partners'/shareholders' compensation $ _____
- Associate lawyers' compensation .. $ _____
- All other payroll .... $ _____
- Rent .... $ _____

  ALL OTHER EXPENSES
(including supplies, travel, postage, telephone, professional services, client disbursements written off, depreciation of furniture and fixtures, etc.) .... $ _____

8. How much office space does your firm occupy? .... sq. ft. _____

NET WORTH

9. What was the amount of unbilled time (work in process) at your regular hourly rates at the end of December 31, 199X?
(Do not include *pro bono* work) .. hrs. _____

10. What was the amount of time written off (either as unbillable or through reduced rates) during the year? .... hrs. _____

11. What were the "clients' costs advanced," outstanding at the end of December 31, 199X? .... $ _____

12. What was the amount of billed accounts receivable at the end of December 31, 199X? .... $ _____

HOURLY RATES/SALARIES

13. Which one of the choices below <u>most closely</u> describes how your hourly rates are determined? *(check only one)*

Based on costs ☐   Competition ☐   Arbitrary ☐   Other ☐
(if "Other" describe: _____)

14. This question compares attorneys' salary rates, billing rates, and billable hours by years of experience and position in the firm.
(please fill in the boxes)

	Years in Position	Average Hourly Rate ($)	Annual Avg. No. of Billable Hrs.
Partners/ Shareholders	1–4 years		
	5+ years		
Associate Lawyers	1–2 years		
	3–4 years		
	5+ years		

FIGURE 2.1   Law Firm Economic Survey, *continued*

15. Who determines employee compensation? *(check all that apply)*
- All partners .... ☐
- Committee......................... ☐
- CEO .... ☐
- Managing partner................ ☐
- Other:............................... ☐

16. Do you bill clients for these expenses?

	YES	NO
Photocopy time	☐	☐
Telephone time	☐	☐
Clerical time........................	☐	☐
Incoming fax charges.............	☐	☐
Outgoing fax charges	☐	☐

Are above billed at: cost? ☐ marked up? ☐
if marked up, what percentage? ☐

MANAGEMENT

17. Does your firm hold partner/shareholder meetings?
Yes ☐   No ☐
How many times per year?.......... ☐

18. Does your firm have a written business plan?
Yes ☐   No ☐

19. Does your firm utilize a formal cash flow statement?
Yes ☐   No ☐

20. How many attorneys do you expect to ADD to your firm in 199(X + 1)? ... ☐

21. How many do you expect to DROP from the firm in 199(X + 1)?.... ☐

22. How many attorneys do you expect to ADD to the firm in the next five years?............................. ☐

23. On average, how many years does it take a first year associate to be admitted to partnership on a normal track?.... yrs. ☐

MANAGEMENT INFORMATION SYSTEMS

24. Are you currently using a computer system?
Yes ☐   No ☐

25. Who manages your computer system? *(check all that apply)*
- Attorney .... ☐
- Bookkeeper....................... ☐
- Systems manager................. ☐
- Office manager .... ☐
- Outside consultant .... ☐
- Other: .... ☐

26. Are you using your computer system for: *(check all that apply)*
- Word processing .... ☐
- Time and billing................... ☐
- Accounts receivable .... ☐
- Calendar and docket control......... ☐
- Document management............. ☐
- Payroll .... ☐
- Accounts payable .... ☐
- General ledger .... ☐

27. How has the system effected staff size? *(check only one)*
- Reduced it .... ☐
- Increased it .... ☐
- No change........................ ☐

GROWTH

28. In the last year, how has the volume of work changed? *(check only one)*
- Increased .... ☐
- Decreased .... ☐
- Same............................... ☐

29. In the last year, how has staff size changed? *(check only one)*
- Increased .... ☐
- Decreased .... ☐
- Same............................... ☐

CHAPTER 3
Setting Goals

If you don't know where you're going, you might wind up someplace else.

—Yogi Berra

Chapter Checklist   **Identifying Personal Goals**
Identifying Law Firm Goals
Action Plan

It is important to have goals, because only when you have goals can you make plans.

Goals are specific statements describing results that you want to achieve. There is no paucity of treatises and theories defining and elaborating on concepts such as values, missions, goals, and objectives. In keeping with my belief in simplicity, I am going to condense them all into one term in this chapter—GOALS. An example of a personal goal is to retire by the age of sixty and never have to work again. A law firm goal might be to become the largest family law firm by revenue in the city.

Both of these goals are: (1) specific and (2) capable of being evaluated by some objective criterion. Statements such as "to be the best" and "to be proud of my profession" are not specific enough, and by my definition, not truly goals. How will you know when you are the best? Or when you will be proud?

IDENTIFYING PERSONAL GOALS

I once knew a tax practitioner who had a traditional accounting background (business school, accounting firm), and who, after passing the Bar, naturally gravitated to tax law. But after several years, he found himself pushing pencils and not really enjoying his work. When he asked me to consult with him about his practice, he confided in me that his law practice was stagnant, and that he was not happy in his career. My advice began with a simple question. "What do you *want* to do?" I asked him.

He said that he had never really thought about it; he had just drifted into the work he was doing. I suggested that he might

Part I: Creating the Business Plan

want to start a goal-setting process by answering questions that you should also be thinking about. Questions like, What do you want to be when you grow up? You might think this is a ridiculous question, one that is only asked of children or young adults, but like my friend above, some people never get around to asking it. What is it about the law that you really like? What don't you like? Do you have a passion for the law that keeps you practicing it?

What kind of firm or practice do you want—small, medium, or large? Do you want to specialize or do you like being a general practitioner? Are you a full-service law firm or a "boutique"? Contingency or fee-based? Do you seek business or individual clients? Sophisticated or unsophisticated clients? What do you want your geographic orientation to be—local? regional? national? What about your image—high-profile or understated? High-powered or low-key? Do you want to be viewed as progressive or traditional? Do you want to optimize profits or lead a more relaxed lifestyle?

It is never too late to set goals, and you can never revise or restate them too many times. The more thought you give to your goals, the better. You need to decide what you want to be. You need to be realistic. And then you need to stay focused on whatever you decide.

A now-well-known psychologist—let's call him Bill—was a college instructor making under $20,000 per year. Deciding to change his life and to make more money, he wrote his desired annual income goal—$125,000—on the bathroom mirror in lipstick. Every morning and every evening he looked at the mirror and focused on his goal. Soon he saw an opportunity to share his knowledge of people and what makes them tick with corporate clients. He began actively marketing himself to corporations, and his growing business was soon bringing in $40,000 annually.

Still looking at his mirror and focusing on his goal, Bill decided to expand even more. He wrote a general-interest psychology book on his own and began looking for ways to let people know about it. He investigated advertising in large publications like *Reader's Digest* but found the ad rates much too expensive. But he did not give up looking for opportunities to publicize himself and his book. One day, he met a writer at a party who was intrigued by the psychologist's ideas. After an interview, the writer wrote an article about psychology for the *National Enquirer*, mentioning Bill and his book.

The book soared in popularity, and Bill went on a speaking tour to promote it. Only when his income reached $400,000 did he erase the lipstick from the mirror.

IDENTIFYING LAW FIRM GOALS

The smaller the firm, the more intertwined the personal goals of the lawyer and the goals of the firm become. For the individual

Chapter 3: Setting Goals

lawyer to endorse the firm's goals, those goals must also support the individual's goals. It works both ways. Let's say that the majority of a firm's four partners believe that their mission is to help the indigent and the needy. Does that mesh with the desires of lawyer A, who has a large family and who is concerned only with taking home the largest draw possible? Probably not, and eventually the partnership will have to resolve the conflict. It is important to find out in the planning stage whether the personal goals of the principals are consistent with the firm's goals. The two need not be the same, but they cannot be in conflict with each other.

Personal goals usually deal with things like money, retirement, time with family and/or to travel, personal satisfaction, etc. Law firm goals typically include topics like firm size, revenue/profits desired, personnel size, firm image, practice areas, type of clients, etc.

Approach this goal-setting procedure in two parts. First, have each lawyer and staff member answer a list of thought-provoking questions about themselves personally and about themselves professionally (see Figure 3.1: Personal Goals Questionnaire). This should be done *before* the first planning meeting. The purpose is to get the participants to start thinking about their goals and how they fit into the bigger picture of the firm. The answers to the questions are to remain personal—no disclosure to the other participants. People should be encouraged to share this process with their families or others closely involved in their lives since they have something at stake here too. Solo practitioners *especially* will want to consult their spouses or significant others, since unknown or contrary goals can quickly lead to tension and conflict in a relationship.

Then, have the same individuals answer the questions about the firm itself (see Figure 3.2: Law Firm Goals Questionnaire). By thinking about and answering these questions (adding or subtracting questions as needed), each person will have given some thought to the major areas of concern to the firm, so that when the whole group first meets to delineate and refine the company's goals, the groundwork has been done.

The priority, then, of the group's first meeting is to agree on the firm's goals. Simply go topic by topic down the firm questionnaire, discuss the various responses and opinions, and write the final, agreed-upon goal statements. If you need to take more than one meeting to do this, so be it. Everyone needs to understand and agree to the firm's goals before you can proceed. However they are framed, the goals belong to you and the firm—they are your own story; they are your dreams; they are your future!

By going through this procedure, you will discover very quickly if you and your partners see eye to eye on the direction of the firm. Only when the "big picture" of your practice's goals is clearly defined can you take advantage of the opportunities that

Part I: *Creating the Business Plan*

FIGURE 3.1   **Personal Goals Questionnaire**

> This questionnaire is for your benefit and will not be disclosed to anyone else. The purpose of answering these questions is to help you analyze your personal goals and put them into context with the goals of the firm. We encourage you to share this process with input from your spouse or significant other.
>
> 1. What have been the most satisfying and the least satisfying work-related activities in your life?
> 2. What have been and what are the most satisfying and the least satisfying aspects of your personal life?
> 3. How does your work-related life currently impact your personal life?
> 4. Do you feel that you spend enough time with your family and friends?
> 5. Do you plan to retire? When?
> 6. How much money are you currently making? Do you want to make more? How much more?
> 7. What aspect of the practice of law has been the most satisfying to you?
> 8. What would you like to be doing in your work-related and non-work-related life in five years?
> 9. Why did you go to law school?
> 10. What percentage of the goals you wanted to achieve by practicing law when you graduated from law school have you actually achieved?
> 11. Which field of law interests or satisfies you the most?
> 12. How much time (by percentage) do you spend in that field?
> 13. What part of your law practice do you love and what part do you hate the most?
> 14. What other complaints do you have about your practice?
> 15. What one thing would you change to make your law practice more satisfying? Why haven't you changed it? How can you go about changing it?

will inevitably come along to move you down the road to success. And because of this planning process, you will tend to become more focused, and once focused, you will be more likely to see and understand and take advantage of the opportunities that pass in front of you, just like our psychologist with his lipstick.

Once your vision of your overall goals is clear, it is time to work on your marketing and financial plans.

Chapter 3: Setting Goals

FIGURE 3.2   **Law Firm Goals Questionnaire**

> This questionnaire deals with your view of the activities and the performance of the firm. The purpose of answering these questions is to help determine problem areas and areas of opportunity for the practice. These answers should be shared with all involved in the planning process.
>
> 1. What is the image of this firm? Should the image be different? How?
> 2. What are three of the firm's strengths? Three weaknesses?
> 3. What are the major threats facing the firm?
> 4. What are the main opportunities facing the firm?
> 5. What current and future trends are affecting or will affect the firm?
> 6. Where is the firm headed for the next five years? Where should it be headed? What changes within the firm will need to be made to accomplish this change in direction? Should the firm add/delete practice areas in the next five years?
> 7. Do you think the firm is too large, too small, or just about right in size? What is the optimum number of lawyers for the firm presently and in five years?
> 8. How would you rate (good, average, bad) the firm in terms of its:
>   - Personnel policies/procedures
>   - Financial performance
>   - Administration/management practices
>   - Clients/marketing activities
>   - Practice development
> 9. What improvements can you suggest for the firm in each of these same areas?
>   - Personnel policies/procedures
>   - Financial performance
>   - Administration/management practices
>   - Clients/marketing activities
>   - Practice development

ACTION PLAN

- Have all the people involved in the planning process answer the Personal Goals Questionnaire and the Law Firm Goals Questionnaire in this chapter. Modify as needed.
- Have your first planning meeting and write down the firm's goals in less than three pages. Have more than one meeting if needed.

CHAPTER 4
Creating the Marketing Plan

Marketing is an attitude, not a department.

—Phil Wexler

Chapter Checklist **Components of a Marketing Plan**
More Thoughts About Marketing
Action Plan

Forget all the textbook definitions of marketing that you may have read over the years. It is really very simple: *Marketing means getting and keeping customers or clients.*

Any action that helps do that is marketing or, as some call it, practice development. Some, like advertising, are obvious, while others are not. Leading seminars, public speaking, publishing brochures and newsletters, how your office staff answer the phone, handling complaints, client relations, differentiation, quality—these are all marketing considerations, since they help you or hinder you in reaching out to your prospective clients and in holding on to their business once you have it.

Since the marketing activities just mentioned—and many more—can cost a significant amount of money, it is crucial that marketing be considered very carefully and *that it be planned*.

Unfortunately, it is very common for law firms to make decisions to spend money on advertising or brochures or other items on the spur of the moment. Usually, a partner has just seen an ad by a rival firm, or reads an article about the latest marketing gimmick in a legal publication and decides to commit scarce resources to try out the idea. This is not the way to do it! A well-thought-out marketing plan takes into account the firm's goals and direction (established in the previous chapter) and considers all the marketing options in coming up with the most appropriate strategy. There are, of course, unforeseen opportunities that may come up, but they can be judged against the marketing plan and incorporated or dismissed.

Part I: Creating the Business Plan

A marketing plan is one of the main components of the business plan and is usually created and revised on an annual basis, although it can be reviewed at shorter intervals if it needs changing.

COMPONENTS OF A MARKETING PLAN

A simple marketing plan answers these questions:

1. What is our current situation?
2. What are we trying to accomplish?
3. Who are our target customers, or clients?
4. What is our strategy for reaching them?
5. Who does what, when, and for how much money?
6. How will we know if we are successful?

Let's look at these marketing plan elements in depth.

What Is Our Current Situation?

This is an assessment of your practice and of the legal market that pertains to you. It is the where-have-you-been, where-are-you-now, and who-are-you-now analysis. It is both qualitative and quantitative in terms of the type of information required.

The qualitative side is comprised of opinions and attitudes about marketing issues held by the lawyers and staff of the firm. The relevant issues and questions to be answered include: What services do you offer? How are you providing those services? What is the need for those services? Are those needs changing? Who else provides those services (competition)? What do you think your strengths and weaknesses are? What are the strengths and weaknesses of your competition? Are you likely to face competition from large firms or from smaller, boutique firms? What are the practice area trends in your community or in general? The trends apparent in our economy, both national and local, allow you to spot opportunities and shift practice areas. For example, because of the real estate slump in many areas of the country, firms are getting more involved in foreclosures. The same can be said for bankruptcies, services for the elderly, and environmental law. Each region or sub-region will have its own peculiarities, strengths, and concerns.

The quantitative information is more statistical and factual: Can you identify the sources of referrals and business? What are they and what percentage of your overall business do they contribute? Can you identify the type of clients you currently have by number and by percentage? How about by practice areas? Are they individuals or businesses? Can you identify the clients that provide the bulk of your revenue? Can you identify all your fees by source? How has your volume of work changed in the last year: Increased? Decreased? How about your revenue? Your staff size? How much advertising have you been doing and where? What was the response to those ads? What were the total fees and/or contingency recoveries collected for the last three to five years?

Go to sources such as the American Bar Association and your state and local bars for law firm statistics and general information about current conditions in the legal industry. The *Martindale-Hubbell Legal Directory* and other similar directories can help you research questions such as, How many firms are there in your area? How many individual lawyers? What percentage are small, medium, or large?

Much of the firm-specific information can come right out of the accounting and billing records that you have already gathered or noted in the Law Firm Economic Survey in chapter 2. To help you with a framework for completing your situation review, I have created a Marketing Situation Questionnaire in this chapter (see Figure 4.1). Have each lawyer fill out whatever is appropriate for him or her. Include staff personnel to bring in their point of view about issues that they are knowledgeable about. This valuable information can then be summarized and shared during the planning meetings. A clearer picture about your firm's current situation will emerge, and the steps you need to take to change your situation will become more evident.

What Are We Trying to Accomplish?

What are the marketing objectives that will drive the practice in a specific direction? The quantitative information from the situation review can be your guide. Based on what you already know about your firm, what revenue objectives by client type would you like to achieve? How would you like to shift the practice area balance? What sort of image would you like to project to the world?

This is where you plug in any of the marketing- or practice-oriented goals from the previous chapter. But you now need to do more—you need to come up with specific objectives to help you reach those goals. And those objectives should be quantifiable. For example, a marketing objective could be "to reach out to 1,000 prospective new clients and retain fifteen of those within one year," or "to have at least five articles in regional legal publications mention our name in a positive light."

Refer to the Marketing Strategy Grid (see Figure 4.2) and use the information from the previous section to come up with a few specific objectives for your firm. If you feel that you do not know enough yet, that is all right—create a few objectives anyway, even if they are preliminary. You can revise, refine, and add to them as needed.

Part I: Creating the Business Plan

FIGURE 4.1   **Marketing Situation Questionnaire**

Answer the following questions to determine your firm's current marketing status.

1. Does the firm currently have a *written* marketing plan?
2. Does the firm have a full-time or part-time marketing director?
3. Indicate the percentage of *new* business that comes from the following marketing techniques:

Referral...	_____ %
Seminars/Speeches/Articles	_____ %
Direct mail	_____ %
Firm newsletter/brochure	_____ %
Advertising...	_____ %
Other	_____ %
TOTAL:	100 %

4. Indicate how much is being spent annually on each of the following marketing techniques (list year by year):

Seminars/Speeches/Articles	$_____
Direct mail	$_____
Firm newsletter/brochure	$_____
Advertising..	$_____
Other	$_____

5. What is the annual percentage of total marketing expenses (from above) to revenue?
6. List all clients by type, number, dollar volume, and percentage of revenue.
7. List the top ten clients who have produced the highest revenue for the firm (annually).
8. List the percentage of gross revenue to the law firm from *annual* service clients compared to *one-time* clients.
9. Identify what partners, associates, and staff have done in the past year to help market the firm to existing or potential clients.
10. What has the firm done to determine its clients' current and future legal needs?
11. What type of client or client segment is the most profitable for the firm? (State how "profitable" is defined.)
12. Who will be the clients of the future? What services will they need? Which practice areas correspond to those needs and hold the most promise for future opportunities (i.e., what are the practice areas of the future)?
13. Does the firm have a policy of cross-selling services (promoting other firm services to existing clients)?
14. Which current services should the firm strengthen? Which new services should the firm offer? Which services should the firm eliminate?
15. Who are the three major firms that compete with yours for the same practice areas? What are their strengths compared to your firm? What are their weaknesses?

FIGURE 4.2 **Marketing Strategy Grid**

	Client Type Description: Corporate CEOs in industry X.	
	Objectives:	**Strategies:**
e.g.	Reach 1,000 prospects and retain 15.	Mail 1,000 packets to the prospects by November 1.
e.g.	Receive 5 mentions in local press.	Send press release to local magazine/newspaper editors. Subject: importance of finding outside corporate counsel.

Part I: Creating the Business Plan

Who Is Our Target Customer, or Client?

Who, exactly, are your clients? What businesses are they in? Are there any expected changes in those businesses that could affect *your* business with them? How similar are these clients to each other? How different? What kind of legal work are they looking for? What are their needs now *and what will they be in the future?* What do they think about you and what you offer them? What do they think about the competition and what they offer them? If you do not know the answers to these questions, you need to find a way to ask. A survey form handed or mailed out, a brief interview with new clients, your knowledge of your client base, or even research by an independent research company are all appropriate. The more you know about your clients, the better you will be able to deliver the services that they want.

Using the quantitative information from the first section plus any new data or thoughts, describe your current and *intended* client base.

What Is Our Strategy for Reaching Our Target Audience?

Communications is the nitty-gritty of marketing—some think, erroneously, that communications *is* marketing. The main categories of marketing communications are:

- *Advertising* (sending paid messages via the media). The days of lawyers not advertising are over. It is a question of whether you think it is appropriate for you and which is the best vehicle to get the message out to the target audience. Do not be limited to thinking only of Yellow Pages ads. Trade magazines, radio, and cable television are becoming popular vehicles for legal advertising. Make sure you review the rules of professional conduct in your jurisdiction regarding advertising.
- *Public relations* (getting mentioned in the media, but for free). Get press mentions by becoming an expert on a specific legal subject, and promoting that expertise to newspaper and magazine editors. You can be the one that is quoted when articles are being written. Someone has to do it!

The "other" category comprises whatever is left over:

- *Writing articles in legal publications*. These publications are usually in need of quality articles and will be more than willing to accept your contributions.
- *Speaking at conferences and before industry groups*. Make sure you are speaking to groups of prospective or potential *clients* or colleagues who may refer business to you.
- *Joining targeted trade associations and charitable organizations*. Get involved by joining the membership committee,

where you will meet more people and be recognized as making a contribution to the growth and health of the organization. Or get involved by joining the finance committee or a similar committee that will allow you to learn quickly about the inner workings of the group and place you near the seat of power of the organization.
- *Conducting presentations and seminars.* This is a great way to communicate your expertise, your enthusiasm in a specific field, and your availability.
- *Creating brochures and newsletters.* Realize that while a brochure needs to be created only once (until it is obsolete), a newsletter requires a regular commitment. Brochures can be fancy or straightforward, but their value is not necessarily determined by the cost of production. Either of these promotional materials will put information about your firm directly into someone's hands.
- *Promoting client and law firm referrals.* Satisfied clients, when reminded, are usually happy to make referrals to colleagues, friends, or relatives. Many law firms make referrals of matters about which they feel unqualified or in which there may be a conflict of interest. Make other firms aware of your expertise and availability. Participating in your bar association's activities is an excellent way to become known by other members of the profession.
- *Networking.* Participate in networking gatherings, breakfast "lead-sharing" meetings, etc. But be sure that the participants are potential clients or colleagues who may refer business to you.
- *Preparing mailings.* Prepare mailings to potential clients, in accordance with the rules of professional conduct in your jurisdiction. There is almost an infinite number of sources for names, including mailing-list brokers who do nothing else. If you can identify a target client group, there is undoubtedly a list of those people available. Mailings can highlight a new practice, a new service offered, changes in personnel, a change in the economy—almost anything can be the reason for a mailing. One effective technique is to highlight a change in case law or legislation that may impact your clients. Your analysis or a summary of the change provides a valuable service in addition to creating awareness of your legal services.
- *Cross-selling.* It is a marketing rule of thumb that it is much easier (and less expensive) to sell more services to an existing client than it is to find a new client. Promote other *appropriate* legal services to *all* existing clients.

Realize that the firm's letterhead, building signage, announcements and all other promotional materials are also marketing pieces. They communicate something about you and the firm. Make sure they say exactly what you want them to.

Which marketing strategies and communications techniques will you use to get the word out about your practice and to achieve your objectives?

Let's take the sample objective from section 3 above: "to reach 1,000 prospective new clients and retain fifteen of them." Assume the practice area is personal injury and the target audience is individuals. One strategy would be to utilize print advertising in the Yellow Pages. People who are looking for P.I. lawyers frequently flip through the Yellow Pages looking for an ad that strikes them. The marketing strategy then would read: "Place one ad of XX size in the XX Yellow Pages to run for XX months."

Another target audience with the same objective could be middle-market corporations that need outside corporate lawyers. A different strategy could be to utilize a direct mail campaign to reach the CEOs of these corporations and to convince them of your expertise. A marketing strategy would read: "Create and mail 1,000 direct mail packages by November 1 to corporate CEOs obtained from the XX mailing list."

One firm I know in Los Angeles seeks its clientele from outside its local area; in fact, this firm does no advertising at all in Southern California but spends heavily for advertising in the midwestern and eastern parts of the United States, from which it gets its business referrals. The size of your firm, its practice areas, and its desire to grow are important considerations in the development of your marketing strategy.

The correct selection of media or methods that make up a "marketing mix" is the art of marketing. No one can tell you exactly what will work and what will not. It takes intuition, a hard look at the facts, and experience to do it right. If you are new to marketing, you will just have to try different strategies and pay attention to what works and what does not.

Using the Marketing Activity Checklist (see Figure 4.3), choose the most promising activities to reach your target audience to achieve your specific objectives. One way to represent this visually is to make a grid sheet for each client type like the sample in Figure 4.2 (Marketing Strategy Grid).

How Much TIME, How Many PEOPLE, and How Much MONEY Will Be Required?

This is where you allocate who is responsible for what—whether your marketing will be done internally or through an outside agency or consultant—when it is going to happen, and how much it is all going to cost. (See Figure 4.4: Marketing Action Plan.)

There are advantages and disadvantages to using an outside source such as a consultant or an ad agency to help implement your marketing plan. Outside sources have, or should have, the marketing and communications expertise that you may not. They have staff and resources that most law firms do not have. They

FIGURE 4.3   **Marketing Activity Checklist**

> Marketing for law firms includes many appropriate vehicles or techniques. Here are some alternatives that you may want to consider:
>
> 1. Write articles in your field for legal publications and industry trade journals.
> 2. Speak before appropriate conferences and industry-related groups.
> 3. Join targeted trade organizations.
> 4. Join the professional arm of a charitable organization.
> 5. Participate in networking gatherings.
> 6. Prepare mailings to potential clients.
> 7. Cross-sell to current clients.
> 8. Encourage client referrals.
> 9. Promote law firm referrals.
> 10. Advertise.
> 11. Conduct seminars for clients, prospective clients, and sources of referrals.
> 12. Consider producing a firm brochure or newsletter.
>
> You can use several of these specific techniques in combination to achieve the desired marketing communications result.

also bring an outsider's fresh, unbiased viewpoint to the procedure. This is sometimes the main advantage for firms with strongly held but equally split opinions by partners on how to market the firm. The downside is that outside agencies charge for their services (surprise!), although an hourly fee for an outside creative consultant is usually less than your legal fee.

One way to justify the added expense of hiring an outside firm or consultant to work with you on your marketing is to engage them only for specific tasks that you cannot do. An example would be a firm brochure. You could write it and hire an agency or design firm to do the layout and production coordination. As in many areas of life, it usually pays to hire someone who is an expert in a specific field—even if you have to pay top dollar—and get the job done right.

The money it takes to carry out all the marketing activities can be estimated by your experience or actual price quotations from designers, printers, etc. These marketing expenses must then be plugged into the Cash Flow Expense Form under the "marketing" category (see the next chapter for a complete description of cash flow).

How Will We Know If We Are Successful?

Only by setting up specific marketing objectives that are quantifiable can you honestly evaluate whether you have succeeded or not. Did you receive the five editorial mentions? Did you, in fact,

Part I: Creating the Business Plan

FIGURE 4.4   **Marketing Action Plan**

	Who	What*	By When	Completion
e.g.	Paul Johnson	corporate CEO mailing	Nov. 1	

*Strategies from the Marketing Strategy Grid.

Chapter 4: Creating the Marketing Plan

retain the fifteen new clients? When the objectives are specific, it is easy to know if you have reached them.

Keeping track of the results can be as simple as making notes or check marks on the Marketing Action Plan (see Figure 4.4).

MORE THOUGHTS ABOUT MARKETING

Fear of Marketing

Some lawyers run the other way whenever the word "marketing" comes up. They are afraid of not knowing what marketing is and what to do about it or they feel that marketing is somehow sleazy or distasteful. In fact, lawyers frequently disguise their discomfort by using the term "practice development" instead of "marketing." But with the information presented in this book, along with other reading and investigation, you will learn to recognize and implement sound marketing activities *that make sense for you*.

As for the "sleaze" factor, you will not necessarily be associated with the late-night legal hucksters on television simply because you are advertising your services. Advertising—as well as any other form of marketing—can be accomplished in a tasteful and dignified manner. Since the landmark *Bates* (U.S. Supreme Court) decision, marketing and being a professional legal service provider are not incompatible concepts. Professionalism and sound business practices that include a thoughtful approach to marketing go hand in hand.

Do not forget, *every* contact you have with a client—a letter, a phone call, a report—is a form of marketing, whether you think so or not. Do not be afraid of marketing—take control of it!

Existing Clients

Market to existing clients before looking for new ones. Besides the fact that existing clients are always your best source for additional business, it is cheaper to keep a client than to get a new one. Other industries—the mail-order catalog business is a good example—know this very well. Advertising, buying mailing lists, creating promotional material, paying postage costs, etc., in order to reach prospective clients can be very time-consuming and expensive. Why not go to the clients who already know you and with whom you already have a relationship? They can bring in new clients as well as their own added business. Sometimes, all they need is a reminder from you that you are available to do additional work like estate plans and wills, corporate minutes, judgment renewals, lease negotiations, contracts and options, expungement of prior criminal records, or other areas appropriate to your particular situation.

What Clients Look For

If marketing is getting and keeping clients, then it makes sense to discuss what clients are looking for from a lawyer. The better you know what clients want, the more services you can provide. The clients will be happier, and your relationship will be stronger. Most clients look for five main ingredients in a law firm:

Expertise in the area of specialty. Do you have the knowledge and ability to advocate the client's interests?

Knowledge of the client and his or her business. Do you have hands-on knowledge of the client's business or industry so that you can offer the best advice based on the client's situation?

Imaginative advice. Clients appreciate advice that offers aggressive and creative approaches to business problems. Today we call this being *proactive* to client circumstances. This creates an even stronger bond between client and lawyer. On the other hand, if you are merely reactive, the client may believe that you are only a technician, and a technician is a commodity that can be changed based on pricing of the service, school credentials, and size of firm, among other factors.

Responsiveness and communication. Dealing with the client in a prompt, timely manner, without having to be pushed, is essential to retaining client loyalty. The more organized and businesslike your practice is, the more responsive you will be. Clients want to feel important. The client will feel like a second-class citizen if he or she has to wait for services for a long time or if services that were promised at an earlier time are delayed. In the long term the client will deal only with providers who act as though they believe that each client is important. Clients also appreciate communication or explanations that do not make them feel stupid or unknowledgeable.

Value. Are your rates reasonable? Does the client receive good value for the money charged? Does your service contribute to the client's bottom line by either saving money or making money?

One of the main goals of marketing is to make the prospective or current client aware of you and to make him or her believe that you have more of the above ingredients than your competitors.

Differentiation

Your ability to differentiate yourself from your competitors will be a key reason for success or failure in acquiring clients. There are three main avenues for differentiation:

Quality. Quality has always been a key factor in the purchase of goods and services, and it is especially important in a tough economy. Do you provide the best legal services you can? Do your services meet the expectations of your clients?

Reliability. Do what you say you will do, in the time frame you establish. Explain the process to the client and demystify the judicial system so that the client will know what to expect. Tell the client immediately if and when unexpected events occur and what the events mean to the overall objective of the client and the game plan previously established.

Service. This is probably the single most important factor differentiating one firm from another. Most lawyers are reasonably competent to handle the matters they take on. The demarcation comes in the amount of time the lawyer is willing to spend on a given matter and the communication process, which allows the client to know that the lawyer is working effectively on his or her behalf. How quickly do you return telephone calls and respond to letters? If you are unable to respond because you are in court, preparing for another client, on vacation, or otherwise unavailable, a secretary, paralegal, or other associated lawyer must respond quickly. The response may be nothing more elaborate than saying that you are presently unavailable and will return the call or letter by a certain date. If the need of the client is such that an immediate response is necessary, the lawyer's office should make other arrangements to resolve the matter.

Handling Complaints

A specific part of service, and another element of marketing, is the handling of complaints. Here is what you should do when this client-relations problem crops up:

Log the complaint. This helps determine whether there is a steady or consistent pattern that needs to be dealt with. Frequently, one problem in isolation, even if repeated, may not make us aware of a pattern that needs further treatment.

Look into the problem. Determine all the relevant facts. If the issue relates to billing, do not send another statement until the issue is cleared up; that would only compound and confuse things further. If the bill is the issue, you must determine whether further work is to be performed before the matter is settled.

Respond to the client. Tell the client you are reviewing the matter and will respond to him or her by a certain date. If you take longer than expected, call the client and tell him or her that you will be later than expected, but that you will respond by X, a new target date. Do not let the client believe you are ignoring the client's concern, or that you are too busy to handle the matter, or that you do not care about money (if the billing is in question).

This latter perception may permit the client to further delay payment of future bills.

Determine the solution. The solution must be perceived as fair by the client, and it must be consistent with previous firm policies. There should also be a way for the client to "save face," to be reassured that his or her concern was legitimate even if it could not be handled in the way that the client desired.

Communicate and explain your decision. Even if the response is adverse to the client, he or she must understand the basis of the decision; this may be the only way to preserve the goodwill of the client.

Follow up. Has the matter been resolved to the satisfaction of the client? If the answer is yes, the follow-up will reinforce goodwill created by a satisfactory response. If the answer is no, determine what problem still needs to be addressed. If it can be resolved, do so quickly.

Complaints can be a learning as well as a marketing ("keeping the client") tool; you can find out if there is a gap between what you are promising—as perceived by clients—and what you are delivering.

ACTION PLAN

- Have all the key planning people go over the six elements of the marketing plan and answer the six corresponding questions as completely as possible. To help you do this, review the Marketing Activity Checklist (Figure 4.3), and fill out the Marketing Situation Questionnaire (Figure 4.1), the Marketing Strategy Grid (Figure 4.2), and the Marketing Action Plan (Figure 4.4).
- Create your marketing plan. It need not be more than three or four pages long. Modify the forms in this book as needed.
- Allocate the resources (time, money, people) to carry out the marketing plan.
- Hire outside professionals—ad agency, PR agency, design firm, marketing consultant—if needed. (Make sure you add the expenses to the cash flow plan as described in the next chapter.)
- Monitor every marketing activity to evaluate its effectiveness.

CHAPTER 5
Creating the Financial Plan

My difficulty is in reconciling my gross habits with my net income.

Errol Flynn

Chapter Checklist
Key Financial Terms
Introduction to Cash Flow
Creating the Collected Revenue Cash Flow Form
Creating the Paid Expenses Cash Flow Form
Creating the SUMMARY Cash Flow Form
Congratulations!
Action Plan

The most important element of the business plan is the financial plan. Ironically, this is the step that most firms spend the least amount of time on. The financial plan is the true guide to the firm's success or failure.

The basis of a financial plan is the historical facts of the business up to the point of making or revising the plan. What the revenues and expenses have been comprise the firm's financial history. The natural tendency is for history to repeat itself, and therefore, for the firm to continue along as it always has. But, because you are reading this book and starting to think about planning, you are probably not satisfied with your performance history to date. You probably want to improve your firm's and/or your personal financial situation. History tends to repeat itself, yet those who are mired in the past will never move ahead.

But history does not necessarily *have* to repeat itself—the act of planning can create new directions and effect substantial improvements in a firm's finances. The solution is to take the facts of the past but change some of the assumptions and alter some of the financial and marketing elements to affect the future. Or to put it another way, the financial plan begins with the history of the firm's performance and allows you to take steps that will positively change the future.

Part I: Creating the Business Plan

So what exactly *is* a financial plan? What does it look like and what does it do? Although it could involve many kinds of charts, budgets, and statements, the simplest and most powerful plan of all—and the only one that really counts in a professional service business like a law firm—is the cash flow statement. The cash flow statement is a three-page schematic or document that spells out exactly where and how the firm will spend its money in the next twelve months. The cash flow statement (also called a cash flow budget, a statement of cash, or a forecast) is a *forecasting* tool that is the key to financial planning for lawyers.

The main principle to keep in mind for a cash flow plan is KISS: Keep It Short and Simple. As mentioned before, unless the process is simple, it will not be used. The key is to make a chart that is no more than three pages long: One page projects the firm's *revenue,* one page projects the *expenses,* and the last page summarizes the previous two. No long treatises, no binders, no colors. Just three one-page charts, with supporting data, if desired. For examples of these charts, filled in with information from a hypothetical firm, see Figures 5.1, 5.2, and 5.3 in this chapter.

A cash flow schematic or form can be created in a number of ways. Use any standard spreadsheet computer program (WordPerfect, Excel, Quatro, Lotus, etc.), create your own form with the WordPerfect 6.0 or 5.1 "Tables" feature (Alt F7), or simply copy the blank forms in this book and fill them in.

My plan for the rest of this chapter is to take the forms, break them down row by row, and help you understand how to fill them out. By the end of this chapter you should be able to take the three blank forms in Appendix A—along with the financial information you have already gathered and some careful consideration—and fill out your own cash flow statement.

The amount of time you spend on this planning process will depend on how precise you want the cash flow budget to be. I suggest that you not worry about preciseness, especially the first time you prepare the plan. An error factor will always exist; our world is not perfect, and you will not be perfect the first time you use this process. It gets easier with time and experience.

But before we do that, let's back up to learn a little more about the world of financial accounting.

KEY FINANCIAL TERMS

The financial world has its own language, and while this book is not a financial accounting primer, a working knowledge of the main terms and their definitions will be helpful to you. More definitions can be found in the Glossary in the back of this book.

ACCOUNTS PAYABLE: Money you owe others (usually expenses) that you have not yet paid out.

Chapter 5: Creating the Financial Plan

ACCOUNTS RECEIVABLE: Money owed to you for work done that has been billed but not yet received.

ACCRUAL VS. CASH ACCOUNTING: Accrual records reflect income irrespective of whether cash has been collected. In other words, accrual accounting reflects billings, work in progress (work partially done but not yet billed), and accounts receivable (work billed but not yet collected). Cash accounting, on the other hand, reflects only collections, never billings or work in progress. Almost all small law firms operate on a cash basis, i.e., accounting for cash as it comes in and goes out. Larger law firms maintain both cash and accrual records.

AGING: Refers to analyzing how long a client has owed you money for work performed and billed; shows how old each billing is (see also Figure 5.1 and the Accounts Receivable Aging forms in Appendix B).

EXPENSES: Expenses are uses of the firm's cash; they reduce the cash available. These are all the checks written or charges made for salaries, rent, taxes, supplies, utilities, insurance, etc.

FINANCIAL STATEMENTS: These are reports that summarize the results of a business's transactions during a specific period of time. There are three basic reports or statements that you need to be aware of:

1. *Balance Sheet.* This is a breakdown of the assets and liabilities of a business as of a certain date. It is a static measure or a snapshot of the firm at one moment in time. The balance sheet, in the context of a professional practice, is generally not very important. It does not give any indication of where the business is going. A law firm is not capital- or equipment-intensive; the real assets of the firm, its people, are not balance sheet items.

2. *Cash Flow Statement.* Cash is the grease that makes the wheel turn; without enough of it at the right times, your whole business grinds to a halt. While income statements and balance sheets do provide valid information, the cash flow statement is the most important working document for a law firm as well as for any other business.

   A business needs a cash flow statement because of the time differential between the expenditure of funds and the receipt of cash revenues. This cash-back-to-cash cycle takes time. Before the first cycle is concluded, the second cycle has started. Thus a business needs additional cash to keep the firm operating and must plan for cash flowing both in and out. This is true even in cases where advance, initial retainers are received. Such retainers ease your plight or shorten the cycle, but they do not eliminate this overlap of cycles.

3. *Income Statement.* The income statement—also called the profit and loss statement, or P&L—is moderately important. It tells you how well the firm did financially for a given period of time (see example in Appendix C). Using the accrual (vs. cash) method of accounting, the income statement tells how much revenue has been billed, how much expense has been accrued, and how much net income or profit resulted. The Income Statement is usually prepared on a monthly, quarterly, and annual basis. This statement, however, does not tell us how much cash was collected or was spent. That is done by the cash flow statement.

Part I: Creating the Business Plan

INCOME AND PROFITS: These are two different terms frequently used to mean the same thing in accrual accounting; they have little relevance to small law firms. They both refer to what is left over after expenses are subtracted from sales or revenues. But most professional service businesses are operated on a cash basis. This figure, if it is positive, is usually taken out as a lawyer's salary or draw. (I do not want to confuse the issue with "gross" or "net" profits at this point; but if you are interested, the profits I am talking about here are net profits after federal income taxes are paid.)

REVENUE: Revenues are any sources of cash to the firm; they increase cash available. For lawyers or other professional service providers, the revenue that matters is the revenue that is collected, not billed. It is the fee or recovery that has actually made it through the door that counts.

INTRODUCTION TO CASH FLOW

Let's follow a calendar time line to see how the cash really flows—or slows to a trickle. On days 1 to 30, you perform legal services such as negotiating and writing a contract for your client. On day 30, if you are paying attention to the lessons of this book, you will send out your billing statement to the client. In the meantime, between days 1 and 30, you have expenditures connected with this matter, such as rent, salaries for secretarial and other staff, insurance, etc. Somewhere between day 31 and day 120—let's make it day 63—the client sends you partial payment. On day 48, you start to work on another matter for that client. This matter, for example, is a breach of contract trial that requires the expenditure of additional costs including more rent, more salaries, etc. At the end of the trial, you send out a new statement to the client even though you have yet to receive full payment for the first task. Thus, there is a lag in the cash-back-to-cash cycle.

The cash flow plan is not a historical document to be preserved for posterity in firm files. It is an ongoing management tool that requires constant updating as new information becomes available from the operations of the firm. It is a financial guide that a manager uses to plan for profits by prioritizing, anticipating, and allotting the revenues and expenditure of funds. Cash flow analysis is the most important management tool at your disposal for contemplating future activities and controlling the firm's financial affairs.

You need to concern yourself with the cash flow statement on a weekly, if not daily, basis. The cash flow statement covers a period of twelve months into the future. It should be revised at least monthly so that you can alter directions and spot problem areas when things do not go as you have planned. I call this a rolling twelve-month cash flow budget—every 30 days you knock off the oldest month, make appropriate revisions, and add a new month at the point furthest out in time. (Figures 5.1, 5.2, and 5.3

Chapter 5: Creating the Financial Plan

cover a twelve-month period. When you become more comfortable and proficient with this kind of planning, I suggest you extend the process to eighteen months.)

CREATING THE COLLECTED REVENUE CASH FLOW FORM

The first part of the cash flow statement describes the "inflow," or revenue coming into the firm. To start creating the elements that will become the completed Revenue Cash Flow Form (see Figure 5.1 and the blank form in Appendix A), assemble all the financial facts you have gathered as described in chapter 2. For this part you will need all the revenue information available to you. (See also chapter 9, "Other Methods of Determining Revenue," for related information.)

Let's start with row #1: "Cash Retainers Collected for General Account."

Row #1

CASH FLOW—COLLECTED REVENUE	Jan	Feb	Mar	Apr	May	Jun	Jul	Aug	Sep	Oct	Nov	Dec	Total
Cash Retainers Collected for General Account (not Trust Account)													

One source of "cash inflow" is cash retainers (cash includes checks). Cash retainers are split into two parts: the "nonrefundable retainer" that is given for the privilege of having access to you and that goes into your general account, and the remaining portion, which is considered an advance payment for work to be done and which is put into a client trust account. Let's look at the nonrefundable portion of the cash retainer. Note that there is no precise percentage or amount that is required to be taken as a nonrefundable fee. The amount depends on the size of the retainer, your experience, and your common sense. You should be aware that at the time of this writing, some bar associations are reviewing this issue, and I expect that a rule of professional conduct addressing this issue will soon be developed. Also note that I do not discuss how to handle that portion placed into the client trust account. That portion is not your revenue, not yet earned and, therefore, not to be considered as part of your cash flow or part of your plan.

Look at your historical information and make a total of the nonrefundable portion of your retainers from all of last year (or the most recent twelve-month period). Now evaluate your goals and your marketing strategies and come up with a percentage of change or a new total amount for this category. Take that new *desired* total for the next year and divide the number by 12. You now have the *average* nonrefundable cash retainer you are expecting each month. Using a computer spreadsheet or *a pencil with an eraser,* fill in that number in each square of the first row of the

45

FIGURE 5.1 Cash Flow Projection Form—Collected Revenue

	CASH FLOW STATEMENT	Jan	Feb	Mar	Apr	May	Jun	Jul	Aug	Sep	Oct	Nov	Dec	Total
#1	Cash Retainers Collected for General Account (not Trust Account)	25,000	–0–	15,000	22,000	32,500	7,200	3,200	4,900	3,350	10,000	15,000	45,000	183,150
#2	Transfer of Funds from Trust Account per Client Instructions	100,000	2,000	25,000	100,000	5,000	10,000	–0–	32,000	45,000	–0–	2,500	4,500	326,000
#3	Contingency Fees Collected	–0–	–0–	–0–	–0–	10,000	8,000	33,000	–0–	25,000	4,200	–0–	23,000	103,200
#4	Collected Accounts Receivable	134,000	125,000	112,000	145,000	133,000	122,000	135,000	188,000	189,000	150,000	165,000	130,000	1,728,000
#5	Funds Collected from Sale of Assets	–0–	–0–	–0–	–0–	–0–	–0–	–0–	–0–	–0–	12,500	–0–	–0–	12,500
#6	Miscellaneous Collected Funds	125	–0–	–0–	–0–	1,500	–0–	–0–	4,500	–0–	–0–	–0–	–0–	6,125
#7	Total Operating Funds Collected	259,125	127,000	152,000	267,000	182,000	147,200	171,200	229,400	262,350	176,700	182,500	202,500	2,358,975
	*New Equity Funds Collected													
	*New Debt Funds Collected	5,000	500,000		305,000		230,000	455,000	300,000	110,000	150,000	500,000	2,535,000	2,535,000

Note: A cash flow projection can include 18 months of information. Review and revise the projection on a monthly basis.

Chapter 5: Creating the Financial Plan

Revenue Cash Flow schematic. Do not forget to include the total at the end. Keep in mind that when working with cash flow, you are to fill in amounts *in the month that they are collected or paid out*. Also, fill in *all* the boxes—twelve months' worth—across the page for each row. As you forecast for months further away from the present, the figures may become more conjectural. That is OK, because more information will become available as you get closer in time to those months.

If every business ran with Swiss-watch perfection, you would be done with this section. But business activities have a habit of varying during the year, depending on clients coming and going, staff vacations, etc. So while keeping in mind your experience with seasonality and all the ebbs and flows that you could reasonably expect for your business in the next year, take that same row and, month by month, make adjustments by increasing the amounts for some months and decreasing others. The total at the end should be the same after all this *unless* during the course of this exercise you decide to change your mind about some of your assumptions. That is OK! Thinking about this process—maybe for the first time—will allow you to consider new ideas, new clients, and new strategies that affect your revenue. Just make sure you jot down how and why your assumptions changed. When you are satisfied that this first row of numbers reflects your nonrefundable cash retainers, stop. You have now completed the first step of your cash flow plan. Congratulations.

This is an example of how your first revenue row might look:

Row #1

CASH FLOW—COLLECTED REVENUE	Jan	Feb	Mar	Apr	May	Jun	Jul	Aug	Sep	Oct	Nov	Dec	Total
Cash Retainers Collected for General Account (not Trust Account)	$25,000	–0–	$15,000	$22,000	$32,500	$7,200	$3,200	$4,900	$3,350	$10,000	$15,000	$45,000	$103,150

Now let's move on to Row #2: "Transfer of Funds from Trust Account." This portion of the retainer is the advance payment to be applied against future billings that, according to your State Bar regulations, is to be placed in a client's trust account and is refundable if the work is not completed and the fee not earned. Fee deposits that are placed in the client's trust account represent unearned, advance payment to be applied against expected future fees. This row represents those trust account funds that have been earned during the month in question, irrespective of the source or the time of deposit into this account. When your fee is considered earned, *and* the client has authorized you to withdraw funds from this account for payment of your fees, you are entitled to transfer funds from the client's trust account to your general account. Without both *earning* the fee charged and receiving written *client authorization*, you normally cannot transfer fees.

For safety's sake, client authorization should be specific and should be obtained in writing for each fee payment to be made

Part I: Creating the Business Plan

from the client's trust account. However, some lawyers prefer to get an overall, general authorization rather than contact the client each time. This general authorization should be set forth in writing, and the *written* fee agreement that is signed at the very beginning of the representation should contain it.

Row #2 looks like this:

Row #2

CASH FLOW—COLLECTED REVENUE	Jan	Feb	Mar	Apr	May	Jun	Jul	Aug	Sep	Oct	Nov	Dec	Total
Transfer of Funds from Trust Account per Client Instructions													

Following the same procedure as above, take your information from last year, add your desired changes, your experience, and your best guesses for the future, and fill in the new numbers across this row.

Another revenue source is collected contingency fees. Lawyers working on contingency cases usually handle personal injury, debt collection, workers' compensation, or major antitrust matters. The handling of other matters may also be compensated on a percentage basis. These fees increase your cash in the month in which they are collected.

Row #3

CASH FLOW—COLLECTED REVENUE	Jan	Feb	Mar	Apr	May	Jun	Jul	Aug	Sep	Oct	Nov	Dec	Total
Contingency Fees Collected													

In the same manner as before, take the information you have, make appropriate adjustments for the future, and fill in the boxes in Row #3.

The next source of "inflow" comes from the collection of accounts receivable. Accounts receivable refers to all the money that is owed to you for work done that has been billed but not received, over and above any trust account transfers. In the cash-based method of accounting that I recommend (as opposed to the accrual method), the moment you receive money owing to you and deposit it is the moment that you account for it and declare it as revenue. This is an increase in cash, and it goes into Row #4 in the appropriate box. (For a discussion of specific collection tips for decreasing your accounts receivable and speeding up your cash flow, see chapter 9, "Credit and Collections.")

Row #4

CASH FLOW—COLLECTED REVENUE	Jan	Feb	Mar	Apr	May	Jun	Jul	Aug	Sep	Oct	Nov	Dec	Total
Collected Accounts Receivable													

Chapter 5: Creating the Financial Plan

> **A Special Note to Contingency-Based Lawyers**
>
> You may think that projecting revenues applies only to hourly or other fee-based lawyers, but you can do it too. You know more than you think.
>
> Most contingency matters take anywhere from eighteen months to five years to resolve. Although you may not know exactly when the case will be settled or tried, by looking back into your records and identifying each case, you should be able to estimate when this matter is likely to be resolved and what the likely outcome will be.
>
> You can evaluate how valid the claim is and how much it is worth in terms of recovery. By going through all the cases in the office, you can plot out your expected revenues on the basis of your jurisdiction, the matter, your recovery arrangement with the clients, and your past experience.
>
> This is no less accurate than the method that hourly-based fee lawyers use when they estimate what their revenues will be on the basis of previous history and work expected in the future.
>
> The same goes for the expenses attached to contingency matters. Within weeks of taking the case on, you have probably planned out your strategy. You know how much discovery is involved, how many witnesses to call, how many medical or reconstruction experts to use. This information and your experience should give you a sense of what the case will cost. Plus you can identify the normal office expenses that you have control over, such as salaries and rent.
>
> Contingency-based lawyers can plan too!

Again, take the information you have, make appropriate adjustments for the future, and fill in the boxes in Row #4.

Row #5

CASH FLOW— COLLECTED REVENUE	Jan	Feb	Mar	Apr	May	Jun	Jul	Aug	Sep	Oct	Nov	Dec	Total
Funds Collected from Sale of Assets													

Row #5 is "Funds Collected from Sale of Assets," which represents the money that you collect from the sale of used equipment or other assets, such as a used car, a used computer system, a personal computer, or a telephone system.

Row #6

CASH FLOW— COLLECTED REVENUE	Jan	Feb	Mar	Apr	May	Jun	Jul	Aug	Sep	Oct	Nov	Dec	Total
Miscellaneous Collected Funds													

Row #6—"Miscellaneous Collected Funds"—is for funds received from a variety of other, nondesignated sources, such as the interest on checking accounts or anything else that may be specific to your firm.

Part I: Creating the Business Plan

Row #7

CASH FLOW—COLLECTED REVENUE	Jan	Feb	Mar	Apr	May	Jun	Jul	Aug	Sep	Oct	Nov	Dec	Total
Total Operating Funds Collected													

In Row #7—"Total Operating Funds Collected"—add up the amounts already arrived at for each month, and put the grand total for the year in the far-right box.

You will see two more items after Row #7—"New Equity Funds Collected" and "New Debt Funds Collected." These come from the Summary Cash Flow Form described below. New equity funds represent money to start your new practice or to keep your existing practice on an even keel. This is money that is invested in exchange for ownership—or equity—in the firm. New debt funds are either short-term or long-term loans from a bank, a relative, or another source to whom you will owe these funds. These two rows are not part of the operating revenue because you do not know if you are going to need them yet at this point. Only after you have worked through the Summary will you know if you require additional funds as either new equity or short-term/long-term loans. Although this will be actual cash that you receive, you do not need to account for it on this form; the items are listed here only as reference information. The actual figures are accounted for in the Summary form.

You now have a penciled-in or computer-generated chart that should look something like the example in Figure 5.1, only with *your* firm-specific numbers filled in. This indicates how much cash revenue you are expecting to bring in on a month-by-month basis during the next year. If you are doing this by hand, keep the entries in pencil until after the process is completed and you have finished making adjustments.

CREATING THE PAID EXPENSES CASH FLOW FORM

Expenses are uses of cash, and the next part of the cash flow statement describes this "outflow" of money from the firm (see Figure 5.2 and the blank form in Appendix A). If you have not already done so, assemble all the pertinent financial facts relating to expenses.

Expenses can be predicted with greater certainty than revenues because in a professional practice setting the expenses tend to be limited in kind and tend to be repetitive. The repetitive nature of expenses and the control the professional has over them are the key reasons for the greater certainty in predicting what future expenses will be.

FIGURE 5.2 Cash Flow Projection Form—Paid Expenses

	CASH FLOW STATEMENT	Jan	Feb	Mar	Apr	May	Jun	Jul	Aug	Sep	Oct	Nov	Dec	Total
#1	Employee Salaries	125,000	100,000	113,000	120,000	118,000	119,000	121,000	121,000	119,000	118,500	124,000	123,500	1,422,000
#2	Employee Taxes	12,500	10,000	11,300	12,000	11,800	11,900	12,100	12,100	11,900	11,850	12,400	–0–	129,850
#3	Partners' Draw—Shareholder Salaries	130,000	130,000	130,000	130,000	130,000	130,000	130,000	130,000	130,000	130,000	130,000	260,000	1,690,000
#4	Rent	20,000	20,000	20,000	20,000	20,000	20,000	20,000	20,000	20,000	20,000	20,000	20,000	240,000
#5	Insurance—Health	8,000	7,500	8,000	8,000	7,750	7,750	7,500	7,500	7,750	7,750	8,000	8,000	93,500
#6	Insurance—General	10,000	2,000	–0–	–0–	–0–	10,000	2,000	–0–	–0–	–0–	–0–	4,500	28,500
#7	Insurance—Errors & Omissions	5,000	4,000	4,000	4,000	4,000	4,000	–0–	–0–	–0–	–0–	–0–	–0–	25,000
#8	Marketing & P.R.	1,000	1,000	1,500	1,800	2,000	1,000	3,000	2,500	1,200	1,000	1,300	1,250	18,550
#9	Supplies	3,750	550	1,500	1,650	1,875	600	1,300	2,050	2,150	7,400	2,500	1,600	26,925
#10	Phone/Copy/Fax	2,500	3,000	2,750	3,300	2,750	2,300	2,450	2,200	3,200	3,000	2,800	2,750	33,000
#11	Professional Dues	250	250	250	250	250	250	250	250	250	250	250	250	3,000
#12	Education	1,500	–0–	–0–	1,500	–0–	–0–	1,500	–0–	–0–	1,500	–0–	–0–	8,000
#13	Library	150	150	150	150	150	150	300	–0–	150	300	–0–	150	1,800
#14	Professional Services	2,000	2,000	2,000	2,000	2,000	2,000	2,000	2,000	2,000	2,000	2,000	2,000	24,000
#15	Travel & Entertainments	7,500	2,500	5,000	6,000	5,500	7,000	5,750	6,000	2,500	3,000	2,750	5,000	58,500
#16	Loan Repayment	10,000	10,000	10,000	10,000	10,000	10,000	10,000	10,000	10,000	10,000	10,000	10,000	120,000
#17	Total Operations Expenditures	339,150	292,950	309,450	320,650	316,075	325,950	319,150	315,600	310,100	316,550	316,000	439,000	3,920,625

Note: A cash flow projection can include 18 months of information. Review and revise the projection on a monthly basis.

Expenses include such items as payroll, library, continuing legal education, rent, auto, dues and subscriptions, insurance (errors and omissions, general liability, etc.), telephone, and utilities. In addition to these expense items, "out-flow" includes capital expenditures such as equipment and furniture purchases, but these infrequent expenses are covered on the Summary Chart described below.

Many of the expenses cannot be controlled or reduced once set in place. These items include rent and insurance, although in today's fluid economy, even rent is not as "fixed" as we used to think. However, some items can be reduced, such as library expenditures (you can share a library or use the county law library in your local jurisdiction), payroll (to a more limited extent, especially if you are a sole practitioner), and dues and subscriptions. Savings in these three areas alone can be substantial in many cases. Further, if you know when to anticipate low and high cash flow periods, you can postpone or advance equipment purchases. (For more cash flow tips, see chapter 13, "Tricks of the Trade.")

If you do not have the needed historical facts for filling out the expense cash flow chart, there are industry standards or guidelines that may speed up the process for you. According to a recent study, the expenses of the average law firm can be estimated in the following percentages:

Expense Item	Percentage of Expenses
Staff (incl. paralegals)	45% (not incl. draws)
Occupancy (rent)	17%
Equipment (on Summary Chart)	6%
Malpractice insurance (E&O)	4%
Outside professional services	2%
Library	2%
Marketing & PR	2%

In this example, the total is 78 percent, a high percentage that leaves only 22 percent for the lawyers as draws or salaries. It used to be that operating expenses would only total about 50 percent, leaving 50 percent for the lawyers. Currently, many firms are reporting non-lawyer operating expenses of over 70 percent.

Keep in mind that projected expenses based on industry averages are just that: averages for firms that may or may not be close in nature to your firm. In fact, these averages are usually based on larger firms. Using these averages as anything more than a benchmark or reference point is dangerous.

I have broken out expenses by standard categories. Feel free to modify these headings to reflect your particular needs or to mirror your own "expense chart of accounts."

Chapter 5: Creating the Financial Plan

The single most important (i.e., largest) expense for a law firm is salaries. Salaries are comprised of two categories: employee salaries and partners' draws or shareholder salaries. Row #1 is for "Employee Salaries."

Row #1

CASH FLOW—PAID EXPENSES	Jan	Feb	Mar	Apr	May	Jun	Jul	Aug	Sep	Oct	Nov	Dec	Total
Employee Salaries													

Employee salaries concern employees such as secretaries, receptionists, telephone operators, clerical personnel, etc., but *not* lawyers. Many small firms and solo practitioners are successful in maintaining a low ratio of personnel to lawyers; that is, fewer personnel are required in today's technological environment than at any time in history. In addition, many tasks today can be "outsourced"; that is, there are companies that act as independent contractors and specialize in specific tasks such as accounting, secretarial work, and even lawyering. The advantage of such outsourcing is that you incur expenses only when and as they are required. The disadvantage is that it is sometimes hard to predict when that will be. Outsourcing expenses should be forecasted in reference to the anticipated revenue strategies determined in the Collected Revenue chart already created. By contrast, if you maintain a regular staff, the expenses related to staff salaries are readily known and predictable.

So for Row #1, fill in the anticipated employee salaries using the same procedure as before. Be sure that these figures reflect any changes in staffing due to new marketing strategies, downsizing or growth plans, extra projects, or the need for additional help around vacation time. For example, in a one-secretary firm, when the secretary goes on vacation, the work still needs to get done. You would probably have the expense of one temporary plus the normal pay for the permanent secretary on vacation. Adjust the amounts *in the months in which they will be paid*.

Do the same for the expected employee taxes in Row #2.

Row #2

CASH FLOW—PAID EXPENSES	Jan	Feb	Mar	Apr	May	Jun	Jul	Aug	Sep	Oct	Nov	Dec	Total
Employee Taxes													

Employee taxes are an important category and should be considered separately. Failure to pay payroll taxes is not only a civil offense that carries a stiff fine, but it may also be a criminal offense under certain circumstances. There is no excuse to forget this category and there must be no temptation to "temporarily" borrow the tax money until that expected "check in the mail"

Part I: Creating the Business Plan

arrives. Too many times that check does not arrive and there are no funds available to pay the payroll taxes. This process can be compounded until the "hole" is too big to crawl out of and the professional faces the worst of consequences. In some jurisdictions, such a violation is deemed to be moral turpitude and, apart from civil and criminal penalties, is reason for disbarment.

The tax generally approximates one-third of employee salaries. This is not applicable to partner draws until such time as the draw is converted to salary. The tax does apply to shareholder salaries as and when the salaries are paid.

Now move to Row #3, "Partners' Draw/Shareholder Salaries."

Row #3

CASH FLOW—PAID EXPENSES	Jan	Feb	Mar	Apr	May	Jun	Jul	Aug	Sep	Oct	Nov	Dec	Total
Partners' Draw/Shareholder Salaries													

While the salaries of staff are often fixed (already determined), draws or shareholders' salaries are not, or at least should not be, fixed. "Fixed" expenses are constant and usually do not change regardless of what the firm is doing or not doing. "Variable" expenses can vary with firm activities or decisions.

The single largest expense that *should* be variable is the partner or shareholder's draw or salary (see related Sidebar on page 55 for more about this). Although many lawyers act as though they believe that they are entitled to a particular draw or salary and that this sum should be increased each year, I believe that lawyers must now approach their draw or salary as a variable expense, not as a "given." As in any business, lawyers who "own" their practice should be the last ones to be paid. Whatever is "left over" is available to pay the draw or salary of the lawyer(s). The financial focus of the firm should be on the success of the business, not the enrichment of the lawyer(s) at the expense of the firm. After all, without a healthy business, there will not be any salary to draw!

Fill in the appropriate numbers in Row #3.

Typically, the second largest category of expenses is rent—see Row #4.

Row #4

CASH FLOW—PAID EXPENSES	Jan	Feb	Mar	Apr	May	Jun	Jul	Aug	Sep	Oct	Nov	Dec	Total
Rent													

Usually, rent is a fixed obligation based on a previously signed lease or rental agreement. The only variables are the charges for "escalations" or "pass-throughs" (including "common area maintenance") based on a formula set forth in the lease.

Personal/Professional Expense Hierarchy

An important expense item that has a significant impact on cash flow is the partner draw or lawyer's salary. This is a touchy area for most lawyers, and one's personal style of living and expenses become an important consideration in any successful cash flow budget. To help small-firm and solo lawyers in thinking about what they need to take out of a firm as an owner (or the owner if a solo), I have developed my "Personal/Professional Expense Hierarchy."

The Personal/Professional Expense Hierarchy

Practice Needs	Personal Needs	Savings for the "Valleys"	Savings for emergencies/ retirement	Gravy
$ _____	$ _____	$ _____	$ _____	$ _____

(All figures are per month.)

The Expense Hierarchy shows five boxes for the basic categories of cash expenditures. These boxes, or levels, represent the needs for cash in the order of priority that a solo or small-firm lawyer should consider for the health of the firm and his or her own livelihood.

First come the needs of the practice. This box contains all the expenses associated with the practice of law and the operation of your office. Why is this first? Because without the practice, there is no source for personal needs. For a hypothetical one-lawyer firm, as an example, let's say that number is $8,000 per month.

Second are the lawyer's personal needs as reflected in the partner draw or salary. What are all the expenses required by you and your family to maintain your style of living? This is the box that should be the most flexible; that is, if the practice produces sufficient income, then you can increase the standard of living. But, the better approach is to avoid committing yourself to extensive obligations from which you cannot retrench in time of need. Let's give our hypothetical solo lawyer with a small family $12,000 per month.

The third box is allocated to savings for the "valleys" of the practice. During each month, some funds should be set aside to carry the practice through those leaner times experienced by every lawyer and law firm regardless of size. These valleys are typically *temporary* interruptions of revenues caused either by a transitory shortage of funds by clients or a temporary lull in their legal requirements that shows up as an unsteady flow of funds to the lawyer. Our lawyer puts aside $2,000 during each of six "peak" or fat months.

The fourth box is for personal savings for unexpected emergencies or for retirement. Too few of us are independently wealthy or maintain a second business activity that will provide ready funds for unanticipated uses down the road. Therefore, the better approach is to set aside a small sum each month and forget about it. Without getting bogged down in investment theories, interest rates, and the like, suffice it to say that because of the power of compounding interest, some sort of regular savings of even a small sum of money can grow significantly over several years. A quick rule of thumb is the "Rule of 72." Take an interest rate and divide it into 72. That is how many years it will take for the money to double in amount. Our lawyer socks away $200 per month for ten years.

And the last box is for "gravy." After setting aside funds for each of the above categories, the balance should be considered a bonus. This is the money to reward yourself with a trip, a purchase of something special for you or the business, a speculative investment, a charitable contribution, etc.

So our hypothetical solo practitioner is spending approximately $21,000 per month in the first four boxes. If he or she pulls in, say, $24,000 each month in revenue, then there is an excess of $3,000 per month in "gravy." If, however, our lawyer is collecting only $18,000, then something has to give, and probably it will be the variable partner draw, or box #2.

Part I: Creating the Business Plan

But, even when a portion of the rent is unknown until the end of the year, a very close estimate of the amount that will be due and when the amount will be payable can be figured by referring to your previous experience with the landlord or to the experience of other tenants in the building. This information is readily available. If there are no anticipated changes, fill in the boxes with the same rent amount for each month for the entire year. (For more about reducing your rent expense, see chapter 13, "Tricks of the Trade.")

Fixed costs like rent (occupancy costs) tend to be higher in the West than in other parts of the country because the rates per square foot are greater and the office spaces tend to be larger. Also, the proportion of this expense to revenue is greater because Western law offices tend to use more staff per lawyer.

The next three rows concern insurance.

Row #5

CASH FLOW—PAID EXPENSES	Jan	Feb	Mar	Apr	May	Jun	Jul	Aug	Sep	Oct	Nov	Dec	Total
Insurance—Health													

Row #5 is for health insurance expenses.

Row #6

CASH FLOW—PAID EXPENSES	Jan	Feb	Mar	Apr	May	Jun	Jul	Aug	Sep	Oct	Nov	Dec	Total
Insurance—General													

Row #6 is for general insurance expenses, including general liability, business interruption, fire (at replacement value), office package (replacement of valuable papers), personal property, workers' compensation, and a general umbrella policy.

Row #7

CASH FLOW—PAID EXPENSES	Jan	Feb	Mar	Apr	May	Jun	Jul	Aug	Sep	Oct	Nov	Dec	Total
Insurance—Errors & Omissions													

Row #7 is for errors and omissions (malpractice) insurance. Fill in the appropriate amounts for all insurance costs.

Row #8

CASH FLOW—PAID EXPENSES	Jan	Feb	Mar	Apr	May	Jun	Jul	Aug	Sep	Oct	Nov	Dec	Total
Marketing & P.R.													

Row #8—Marketing and Public Relations—can be a large expense category. Advertising is not cheap and neither are mailings. The old rule of thumb was "Marketing is the first expense to cut when things are tough." I believe in the counterargument that when times are tough and everyone else is cutting back on marketing, *that* is the time to keep your marketing efforts strong. You will stand out from the crowd (one of the purposes of marketing) and establish yourself in the market. My suggestion is to keep your marketing costs somewhere between 1 and 5 percent of total operating costs. However, this rule of thumb is only that—a guideline. It clearly has no relevance when you first open your practice. Then, much of your time and a high percentage of your expenditures will be for marketing.

As before, make sure to figure your payments in the month that they are to be paid out. For example, if you are running an ad campaign through an advertising agency, your expenditure for a November newspaper ad may be due in advance or on a net 30 basis, depending on the agency's policies.

In general, ad agencies tend to charge a monthly retainer plus hourly billing for services rendered on a net 30 basis. Outside expenditures made on your behalf may be billed in advance. Public relations agencies mostly work on an advance monthly retainer. Design studios tend to charge on a project basis, with a 50 percent advance and the balance due on completion or billed net 30.

Row #9

CASH FLOW—PAID EXPENSES	Jan	Feb	Mar	Apr	May	Jun	Jul	Aug	Sep	Oct	Nov	Dec	Total
Office Supplies													

Row #9 is for office or miscellaneous supplies.

Row #10

CASH FLOW—PAID EXPENSES	Jan	Feb	Mar	Apr	May	Jun	Jul	Aug	Sep	Oct	Nov	Dec	Total
Phone/Copy/Fax													

Row #10 is for another large expense category—telephone charges, fax copies, and photocopies.

In a larger firm, photocopying costs can be a major expense. While many firms bill clients for these expenses, sophisticated clients are now objecting. Such clients are saying that such expenses are normal, are part of the overhead of a law firm, and should be included in the hourly or other fee being paid by the client. Therefore, the lawyer should absorb such costs. That opinion is spreading among clients.

Most clients do not mind an increase in the hourly billing rate of $5 to $15. This added revenue usually will create a net increase in revenues even after you have paid for the above-listed cost items. Only special items and large per-item costs should be billed to a client. Such items include a large photocopying job, deposition transcript fees, and similar items. Other, smaller

Part I: Creating the Business Plan

charges should be absorbed by the lawyer to make for better client relations and, therefore, larger revenues.

Row #11

CASH FLOW—PAID EXPENSES	Jan	Feb	Mar	Apr	May	Jun	Jul	Aug	Sep	Oct	Nov	Dec	Total
Professional Dues													

Row #11 is for professional dues. If you practice in a state with an integrated or mandatory state bar participation, you will undoubtedly have to pay annual dues. Fill in the amount(s) in the month that you pay the dues; do *not* spread out the fee over twelve months. As an example, if you reside in California, show payment of dues of $500 to California State Bar in November (when the fee is due) and dues of $300 to the American Bar Association in August.

Row #12

CASH FLOW—PAID EXPENSES	Jan	Feb	Mar	Apr	May	Jun	Jul	Aug	Sep	Oct	Nov	Dec	Total
Education													

Row #12 is for continuing legal education (CLE). Education for lawyers has become big business, and there is no shortage of CLE programs available. In at least thirty-seven states, CLE is mandatory. Some providers charge an annual fee—the California Continuing Education of the Bar, for example, provides a program "passport" for $1,500 payable in January—while others charge on a per-use basis. Or you could set aside a specific sum (e.g., $100 per month) for all educational programs.

Row #13

CASH FLOW—PAID EXPENSES	Jan	Feb	Mar	Apr	May	Jun	Jul	Aug	Sep	Oct	Nov	Dec	Total
Library													

Row #13 is for library expenses. Most publishers are willing to bill lawyers on a monthly basis. Consider this category as constant throughout the year.

Row #14

CASH FLOW—PAID EXPENSES	Jan	Feb	Mar	Apr	May	Jun	Jul	Aug	Sep	Oct	Nov	Dec	Total
Professional Services													

Row #14 covers Professional Services, including accountants, law firm management consultants, marketing consultants, or any other *outside* professionals who provide services to the practice.

Chapter 5: Creating the Financial Plan

Row #15

CASH FLOW— PAID EXPENSES	Jan	Feb	Mar	Apr	May	Jun	Jul	Aug	Sep	Oct	Nov	Dec	Total
Travel & Entertainments													

Row #15 is for official firm travel and entertainment of clients.

Row #16

CASH FLOW— PAID EXPENSES	Jan	Feb	Mar	Apr	May	Jun	Jul	Aug	Sep	Oct	Nov	Dec	Total
Loan Repayment													

Row #16 is for Loan Repayments (principal and interest). Any loans you receive (see the Cash Flow Summary section for details) must be paid back, and with interest. Since this is cash out the door, fill in the appropriate amounts, if any, in the months that the payments occur.

Row #17 is Total Operations Expenditures.

Row #17

CASH FLOW— PAID EXPENSES	Jan	Feb	Mar	Apr	May	Jun	Jul	Aug	Sep	Oct	Nov	Dec	Total
Total Operations Expenditures													

Total the amounts for each month in this row and put the grand total in the lower, far-right box. Congratulations, you are now two-thirds through the cash flow plan; see Figure 5.2 for a sample of a filled-in Cash Flow Expenses form. The remaining chart is the summary.

CREATING THE SUMMARY CASH FLOW FORM

The third and final chart is the Summary Cash Flow Form (see Figure 5.3). It combines what we have already done in the Revenue and Expenses forms with new information and provides an overview of the cash flow for the firm. This is the critical schematic to evaluate on a regular basis to keep on top of the firm's economic health.

Row #1 is titled "Beginning Cash Balance."

Row #1

CASH FLOW— SUMMARY	Jan	Feb	Mar	Apr	May	Jun	Jul	Aug	Sep	Oct	Nov	Dec	Total
Beginning Cash Balance													

FIGURE 5.3 Cash Flow Projection Form—Summary

	CASH FLOW STATEMENT	Jan	Feb	Mar	Apr	May	Jun	Jul	Aug	Sep	Oct	Nov	Dec	Total
#1	Beginning Cash Balance	100,000	(105,025)	124,025	(138,425)	12,925	(221,150)	(269,900)	(62,850)	45,950	3,200	(88,650)	179,850	100,000
#2	Plus: Increases—Collected Revenue	259,125	127,000	152,000	267,000	182,000	147,200	171,200	229,400	262,350	176,700	182,500	202,500	2,358,975
#3	Less: Decreases—Paid Expenses	339,150	292,950	309,450	320,650	316,075	325,950	319,150	315,600	310,100	318,550	316,000	439,000	3,920,625
#4	Ending Cash Balance	19,975	(270,975)	(33,425)	(192,075)	(121,150)	(399,900)	(417,850)	(149,050)	(1,800)	(136,650)	(220,150)	(56,650)	1,451,650
#5	Plus: Short-term Loans Required	5,000	-0-	-0-	5,000	-0-	-0-	5,000	-0-	-0-	5,000	-0-	-0-	20,000
#6	Cash Available	24,925	(270,975)	(33,425)	(187,075)	(121,150)	(399,900)	(412,850)	(149,050)	(1,800)	(131,650)	(220,150)	(56,650)	1,471,650
#7	Less: Equipment Purchases	25,000	-0-	-0-	-0-	-0-	-0-	-0-	5,000	-0-	-0-	-0-	-0-	30,000
#8	Balance of Cash	(25)	(270,975)	(33,425)	(195,075)	(121,150)	(399,900)	(412,850)	(154,050)	(1,800)	(131,650)	(220,150)	(56,650)	1,471,650
#9	Plus: Long-term Loans	-0-	500,000	-0-	300,000	-0-	230,000	450,000	300,000	110,000	145,000	500,000	-0-	2,536,000
#10	Free Cash Flow	(25)	229,025	(33,425)	112,925	(121,150)	(169,900)	37,150	145,950	108,200	13,350	279,850	(56,650)	1,063,350
#11	Less: Minimum Saving Act.	100,000	100,000	100,000	100,000	100,000	100,000	100,000	100,000	100,000	100,000	100,000	100,000	1,200,000
#12	Net Free Cash Flow	(100,025)	129,025	(133,425)	12,925	(221,150)	(269,900)	(62,850)	45,950	8,200	(86,650)	(179,850)	(156,650)	(136,650)
#13	Less: Extraordinary Use of Cash Flow	5,000	5,000	5,000	-0-	-0-	-0-	-0-	-0-	5,000	-0-	-0-	-0-	20,000
#14	Net Free Cash Flow Carryover	(105,025)	124,025	(138,425)	12,925	(221,150)	(269,900)	(62,850)	45,950	3,200	(86,650)	179,850	(156,650)	(156,650)

Note: A cash flow projection can include 18 months of information. Review and revise the projection on a monthly basis.

Chapter 5: Creating the Financial Plan

The beginning cash balance (in the first box of Row #1 in the upper, left corner) is the opening capital account for the first day of the office or practice. This is the amount of money with which you start the practice. If the practice is presently an ongoing venture, then use the "book" cash balance (what is showing in your checkbook) as of the first day of the month when you begin this analysis. Be careful to distinguish between the book cash balance and the cash balance according to the most recent bank statement. These two figures will be different.

The next two rows refer to either an increase or decrease in the cash based on the Revenue and Expense charts you have already done.

Rows #2, 3

CASH FLOW—SUMMARY	Jan	Feb	Mar	Apr	May	Jun	Jul	Aug	Sep	Oct	Nov	Dec	Total
Plus: Increases—Collected Revenue													
Less: Decreases—Paid Expenses													

Simply take the monthly totals and pencil them into these rows—revenue in Row #2, expenses in Row #3.

By adding Row #2 to Row #1, and subtracting Row #3, you now have the numbers for Row #4: the "ending cash balance."

Row #4

CASH FLOW—SUMMARY	Jan	Feb	Mar	Apr	May	Jun	Jul	Aug	Sep	Oct	Nov	Dec	Total
Ending Cash Balance													

To the extent that the ending cash balance will generally be less than the desired working cash balance, you may need to obtain a short-term loan. This is shown in Row #5.

Row #5

CASH FLOW—SUMMARY	Jan	Feb	Mar	Apr	May	Jun	Jul	Aug	Sep	Oct	Nov	Dec	Total
Plus: Short-term Loans Required													

Depending on your comfort level and how much you like to sleep at night, the rule of thumb is that in any new law practice, the principals should have an adequate reserve of cash to cover living expenses for six to eighteen months *if no draws or salaries are available to take out of the firm.* In lieu of such a cash supply or a large enough Ending Cash Balance, you may want to consider a short-term loan.

A short-term loan may be a loan from friends or family; it may be loans on your credit card; it may be a revolving bank loan or

Part I: *Creating the Business Plan*

line of credit. But it is intended to be *short-term,* only long enough to get you over a temporary shortfall in the cash flow of the firm.

The total of the short-term loan and the ending cash balance will produce the total "cash available" for that given period of time. Add Row #5 to Row #4; the total goes in Row #6.

Row #6

CASH FLOW—SUMMARY	Jan	Feb	Mar	Apr	May	Jun	Jul	Aug	Sep	Oct	Nov	Dec	Total
Cash Available													

Next, you need to account for capital expenditures, if any, such as equipment, furniture, redecorating, etc. Consider equipment a variable or flexible element. This should be one of the first items to cut or reduce if the cash flow picture is looking bleak. You could also finance a major purchase to spread the payments over time, delay, the purchase or skip it completely until cash flow is restored.

Row #7

CASH FLOW—SUMMARY	Jan	Feb	Mar	Apr	May	Jun	Jul	Aug	Sep	Oct	Nov	Dec	Total
Less: Equipment Purchases													

The difference between cash available and equipment purchases results in the "Balance of Cash" in Row #8.

Row #8

CASH FLOW—SUMMARY	Jan	Feb	Mar	Apr	May	Jun	Jul	Aug	Sep	Oct	Nov	Dec	Total
Balance of Cash													

If the Balance of Cash is negative in one or more months, then you must look for long-term loans to increase the level of cash.

Row #9

CASH FLOW—SUMMARY	Jan	Feb	Mar	Apr	May	Jun	Jul	Aug	Sep	Oct	Nov	Dec	Total
Plus: Long-term Loans													

Long-term loans are usually either new equity funds or new debt funds. New equity funds are received in exchange for ownership—or equity—in the firm. New debt funds are loans from a bank, a relative, or another source to whom you will owe these funds.

Since these funds are actual cash receipts, you need to account for them on this form. These figures are also noted for reference at the bottom of the Revenue form.

Chapter 5: Creating the Financial Plan

Row #10

CASH FLOW—SUMMARY	Jan	Feb	Mar	Apr	May	Jun	Jul	Aug	Sep	Oct	Nov	Dec	Total
Free Cash Flow													

When you add Row #9 to Row #8, the net result is "Free Cash Flow" in Row #10.

Row #11

CASH FLOW—SUMMARY	Jan	Feb	Mar	Apr	May	Jun	Jul	Aug	Sep	Oct	Nov	Dec	Total
Less: Minimum Saving Act.													

Row #11 is a deduction of cash for savings. Law firm savings take two forms: (1) savings for the "valleys" or lulls of the practice, or for unexpected emergencies in the practice, or (2) personal savings, retirement, or unexpected personal emergencies. This is, of course, a variable use of cash.

Row #12

CASH FLOW—SUMMARY	Jan	Feb	Mar	Apr	May	Jun	Jul	Aug	Sep	Oct	Nov	Dec	Total
Net Free Cash Flow													

Subtract Row #11 from Row #10 and you now have the amounts for Row #12—"Net Free Cash Flow." Although nothing in life is free, this is the cash that is available for your use.

Row #13

CASH FLOW—SUMMARY	Jan	Feb	Mar	Apr	May	Jun	Jul	Aug	Sep	Oct	Nov	Dec	Total
Less: Extraordinary Use of Cash Flow													

But there always seems to be another pull on your hard-earned cash, and Row #13 is the last of them. "Extraordinary Use of Cash Flow" means any extraordinary, specific project like a new computer system, relocating the office, redecorating the office. If you have got the cash, this is the place to use it!

Row #14

CASH FLOW—SUMMARY	Jan	Feb	Mar	Apr	May	Jun	Jul	Aug	Sep	Oct	Nov	Dec	Total
Net Free Cash Flow Carryover													

Part I: Creating the Business Plan

Row #14—the last row—now shows the monthly cash totals for the practice with the twelve-month grand total in the lower right box. The significance of the term "carryover" is that the last number in the first column is the first number in the next column, etc. At any point where you want to stop this schematic and start a new one, any of these bottom-line figures will then "carry over" and become the next period's Beginning Cash Balance.

CONGRATULATIONS!

Congratulations, you have now completed the first run-through of a complete cash flow statement. These figures provide an instant view of the cash flow health of the firm. The lower, far-right box on the Summary form—the grand total of cash for the entire period—needs to be a positive number because you cannot live in a negative cash flow world for long!

By reviewing the Summary form, you will see that the negative numbers, if any, will start showing up in Rows #4 (Ending Cash Balance), #6 (Cash Available), and #8 (Balance of Cash). If, after Row #9, you have not changed these negatives to positive numbers, then your ability to do anything about Rows #11 and 13 is severely restricted.

One of the goals of creating and evaluating a cash flow plan is to spot cash problems coming and adjust the firm's activities so that the cash is always flowing in the right direction, i.e., positive. Any dips toward zero—or even a negative—need to be seriously evaluated. You can and should fine-tune all the rows in these three schematics—and, of course, the firm's activities that give you the figures—so that you end up with positive figures in Row #14 in the Summary form.

The hardest part is over; from now on, as you gain experience with your business and with this plan, the fine-tuning and revisions will get easier and easier. And your guesses about the future will turn out to be much closer to reality. (For the next level of analysis, see Appendix D. The *Budget Recap: Revenue* and *Budget Recap: Expenses* forms go into more depth by allowing you to analyze the projected figures, the actual figures, and the variance, or how far off you were.)

If you do not have the time to do this kind of detailed cash flow work yourself, or if you feel less than proficient with numbers, get someone you trust to put together all the figures and to do the clerical work. An accountant, bookkeeper, trusted employee, or adviser is appropriate. But do not forget that *you* must be involved in the development of all the assumptions that go into the making of this plan, and that you are responsible for all the decisions that result from it.

Remember that this is a working plan—you will never actually *complete* it, but you will continue to revise it, evaluate it, and

Chapter 5: Creating the Financial Plan

learn from its steady use. The remainder of this book will present additional information to help you in thinking about your practice and the cash flow and marketing plans.

ACTION PLAN

- Using the three blank cash flow forms in Appendix A, go through the entire process of filling in the numbers as described in this chapter. Plan to spend as much time as needed for this—it can take many hours or even days to complete.
- Review, adjust, and revise the forms as needed depending on how the figures work out. One of your goals should be to limit or reduce all negative numbers.
- Congratulations. You now have a working cash flow statement—a three-page plan that describes the financial health of your law practice.

CHAPTER 6
Final Thoughts on Planning

Let us all be happy and live within our means, even if we have to borrow the money to do it with.

Artemus Ward
"Science and Natural History"
Artemus Ward in London, and Other Papers, 1867

Chapter Checklist **Executing Your Plan for the First Time**
A Final Word About Planning
Making It Work

EXECUTING YOUR PLAN FOR THE FIRST TIME

You have now prepared—or are on your way to preparing—a business plan for a professional service business (your law firm) with three major elements: the identification of your goals, a marketing plan, and a financial plan. All three elements are dynamically related. The marketing plan identifies specific strategies to achieve your goals. The financial plan forecasts the revenues and expenses that will result from carrying out the marketing strategies to achieve your goals.

Recognize that your first efforts to plan may not be perfect; no one ever took on a new task and executed it flawlessly the first time. Lack of perfection (especially in the beginning) is not a reason to refuse to make the effort to create your business plan. Experience and educated guesses ("best efforts") are the most effective teachers.

The "first pass" of your marketing and financial plans will require modification as experience tells you where you were too optimistic or too pessimistic in your predictions. This is a normal result of this process, and you will get better and become more accurate in your projections as time passes.

Part I: Creating the Business Plan

How can you tell that your plan is working? If you think that you have been making some progress in reaching your goals, here are seven signs to show you if you are right:

1. *Results that are in sync with your planning process.* You will be meeting the goals, required actions, deadlines, and responsibilities outlined in your original action plan.
2. *Performance that parallels projections.* It is not realistic to expect every line of the financial statements to match your projections, but the results as shown in your cash-flow revenues and expenses should be close to your forecasts.
3. *Good communication between lawyers and staff.* Let staff members know you are open to their ideas for improving the business. And be sure to share good news so that they can see the progress being made.
4. *Improved cash flow.* This is the obvious—and some would say, only—indicator of success.
5. *Controlled credit.* Are you up-to-date with your creditors? If not, let them see your improvements or proof that change is coming.
6. *Maintenance of customers.* Are you satisfying your clients? Are you gaining clients or are they hemorrhaging away?
7. *Employee morale.* Staff members know when changes are working. Their morale is an accurate barometer of progress.

A FINAL WORD ABOUT PLANNING

Most people are fearful of change. One of the beauties of planning is that it helps mitigate this fear by giving you more control of those changes that are certain to come. Change is something you can count on; the question is, Do you want to control it, or have it control you?

The hardest part about planning is starting to do it. After the initial struggle to get the ball rolling, it is much easier to keep it going. Remember—a failure to plan is a plan to fail.

MAKING IT WORK

The second section of this book will provide additional techniques for the growth and success of your law practice. Chapters 7 to 13 will cover such areas as the pricing of legal services, handling billing and credit, dealing with banks, handling clients, and running your law office more efficiently. These techniques will be help you to achieve the goals you have set forth in the planning process.

PART II
Techniques for Survival and Growth

CHAPTER 7
Pricing Legal Services

Money isn't important, but it's the only way to keep score.
[author unknown]

Chapter Checklist
Cost-Plus Pricing
Market Pricing
Cost Disbursements As an Element of Pricing
Alternative Pricing Methods
The Use of Non-Lawyers
Price Sensitivity and Raising Rates

One of the most difficult tasks facing any new business enterprise is the setting of the price for its products or services. The practice of law is no different. New lawyers struggle with this concept, and even experienced lawyers are challenged by setting the right fees and prices, especially in a competitive legal and business environment. The following discussion will provide the basis for making a more reasoned decision in determining or adjusting your pricing or billing.

The old standard was the "Rule of Three," which stated that one-third of the fee was meant to cover overhead, one-third was for compensation, and one-third went to profit, or the amount drawn or paid to the lawyers or partners. A quick way to estimate a pricing or billing rate using this rule of thumb has been to take a person's salary or draw and multiply it by three. The total is then divided by the number of hours billed for the year. The result is a rough estimation of the billing rate per hour.

But because of changing economic circumstances, the Rule of Three no longer can be relied on. There are now two basic ways to set legal service prices or fees: (1) cost plus a markup, and (2) market price.

COST-PLUS PRICING

The key to this method is understanding what the cost of running your law practice is. Most firms are finding that their costs are eating up anywhere from 50 to 70 percent of the fees collected. Therefore, going through the process of determining exactly what your firm's operating costs are is well worth the time and effort.

First, determine the annual cost of running your office. This should not be too difficult. In small firms, the costs are available from the check register, and in larger firms, from computerized accounting programs. If no other records are available, look to your tax return for the previous year.

Next, determine the number of hours billed. This number is obtained, first, by reference to your time sheets. In contingency or fixed-fee agreements, time records may not be available, but in order to determine the overhead per hour,[1] records must be kept of time spent even in matters where hourly billing does not apply.

But if there are no time records available, then you need to refer to an effort or workload standard. For example, national bar studies have indicated that the average American lawyer bills approximately 1,500 hours each year. In some of the larger metropolitan firms, the standard expected of associates is 2,000 billable hours; and, in still others, it has moved up to 2,200 hours per year.

A total of 2,200 hours means that the lawyer must bill seven hours per day, six days per week, fifty-two weeks per year—a very demanding workload.

Of course, these are *net* hours billed *after* some hours are "written down" or written off. Client goodwill, learning time that should not be charged to the client, and lawyer inefficiency are examples of reasons for the lawyer to write off hours.

Third, determine the additional hours written off because of bad debt or noncollection of fees billed. Not all billings are collected. Some clients do not pay all or part of the bill. Looking at your past history, determine the percentage of bad debt in your office. Some firms experience uncollected fees as low as 1 to 2 percent, others as high as 12 to 15 percent. The percentage of billings actually collected is also called the "realization rate," i.e., what is actually realized as collected income.

Taking the net hours billed, less any hours allocated to bad debt or uncollected fees, you now have the total number of net billable hours per year.

Now you can calculate the overhead cost of running the firm by taking the annual cost of operating your firm and dividing it by the number of net billable hours.

As an example, let's say a lawyer has a solo practice that costs $100,000 per year in overhead to operate. If he or she bills 1,125 hours (net), then the cost of overhead per hour is $89. This figure may vary from year to year, but the variation will not be significant.[2]

When you know the cost of overhead per hour, you can add an amount to the hourly fee—this is the "plus" part. How much you add will depend on what level of earnings from the practice you want to achieve.

Let's look at the math of our lawyer billing 1,125 net hours again. He or she knows that the annual overhead is $100,000. If the goal is to have income *after* overhead of $125,000, then another $111 per hour must be added to the overhead cost, resulting in a total of $200 per hour of "cost-plus" pricing.

Another way to arrive at the same point in cost-plus pricing is with this formula[3]: Take the office overhead and add the desired compensation. To this subtotal, add an additional 25 percent to cover the amount of billings normally written off and uncollected. The total is the billing or pricing goal.

The pricing or billing rate derived from the cost-plus method should be compared to the competition. If the hourly rate is above what other lawyers are charging, you must look at the costs of your operation and find ways of becoming more efficient and reducing costs. It is axiomatic that you cannot sell services at a rate that is higher than the competition unless there is a perceived difference in the quality of the service being provided.

If the fee is below the "market rate," you should seriously consider raising your hourly fee. This will provide more profit and allow you to save some of the difference (in fees received) for promoting future legal services. With this cost-plus information, lawyers can look at billings in an entirely new light.

For example, if you take *pro bono* cases, you can calculate the exact amount of your contribution by multiplying the hours expended by your overhead-cost-per-hour rate. After all, *pro bono* work will also requires the operation of your office and the services of your office staff.

If you want to promote your legal services by giving a bonus or special discount to a current or prospective client, you will know the level below which you cannot go in your fee arrangement because of the cost factor.

MARKET PRICING

A market-oriented price is based on the fees customarily charged by lawyers in your community or in the same area of specialty practice.

In earlier times, fee schedules were published by local bar associations. These schedules indicated what the standard or average fee was for given types of work and what average hourly rate was being charged in the local community. Such fee schedules have been declared to be in violation of the antitrust laws, and bar associations discontinued the practice.

Today, you can find the average rate or fee by having discussions with colleagues and by learning from clients what other lawyers are willing to charge them in order to get their business.

As with any other service or product, "price" is dependent on supply and demand, among other factors. The greater the demand, the greater the price or fee that can be charged. The greater the supply (or competition from other lawyers), the lower the fee charged. The reverse is also true.

In addition, hourly pricing or billing rates normally reflect a number of factors in the context of the marketplace. Case law and the rules of professional conduct in many jurisdictions require that a lawyer's fee be reasonable. Here are some factors to consider in determining the "reasonableness" of a fee:

- The time and labor required
- The novelty and difficulty of the questions involved
- The skill required to perform the legal service properly
- The likelihood, if apparent to the client, that the acceptance of the particular engagement will preclude other engagements by the lawyer
- The fee customarily charged in the locality for similar legal services
- The amount involved in the controversy
- The results obtained
- Time limitations imposed by the client or the circumstances
- The nature and length of the professional relationship with the client
- The experience, reputation, and ability of the lawyer performing the legal services
- Whether the fee is fixed or contingent
- Awards in similar cases
- The "undesirability" of the case

The fee or billing rate is the "suggested retail price" for legal services. But this market-based, asking-price concept is coming under attack both by the legal profession and by consumers or buyers of legal services. As a result, many variations of fee structures—or discounts—are developing.[4] Here are several alternatives:

- Market fee per hour, less a promotional discount for the first year of work, but not less than cost plus a lowered profit markup
- Market fee per hour, less a promotional allowance based on various factors such as volume or cash discounts
- Fixed or capped fee, where the normal fee is not to exceed a stated amount
- Risk/reward sharing, where an incentive "kicker" is added to a lowered "normal" fee if the results are beyond a stated amount or a predetermined result

In all these hybrid pricing methods, the bottom or ending point is the overhead or the cost of operating the law practice, including a reasonable payment to the lawyer. If the fee dips below the cost, it is obvious that the lawyer is paying for the privilege of representing the client. This may work for a little while in *pro bono* cases, but it will not work in matters that are intended to produce profit.

COST DISBURSEMENTS AS AN ELEMENT OF PRICING

Most matters require that the lawyer advance some costs on behalf of the client. Costs are of two types: external and internal.

External costs include messenger services, filing fees, deposition transcripts, and expert witness fees. These are charges that are external to the operation of the office and relate specifically to the individual client's matter. All firms charge clients for the external costs, usually at the fee charged without a markup.

Internal costs include photocopying, postage, telephone, and fax. Many firms charge clients for these costs *plus* a markup. For example, if the hard cost for copying is $0.075 (7.5 cents), the firm may charge 10 to 25 cents per copy in an attempt to make a little extra money.

More and more firms, however, are absorbing these internal costs. Internal costs should not be a profit center. In the corporate world, they are part of overhead and part of the sales price for the product or service. In the lawyer's world, charging for these costs has become a less acceptable way of raising the fee.

Today, many clients are beginning to object to this not-so-subtle price increase. Competitive pressure is forcing lawyers to look at this issue again. Many are using it as a marketing ploy, telling clients that costs will not be charged except for external fees.

Whichever way you choose to handle this, make sure to discuss the issue at the very beginning of representation.

ALTERNATIVE PRICING METHODS

There are many ways to price your legal services. Here are the predominate methods employed by law firms across the country.

Hourly Rate

Also known as the "time-and-billing rate," this is the most frequently used pricing technique today. The lawyer computes the time expended on a given matter and multiplies that total by an hourly rate. The result is the amount billed to the client for the lawyer's fee. Costs are billed separately as described above. Time is normally computed on the basis of a minimum time unit charged—or minimum billing unit—of 1/10 or 1/4 hour.

An hourly rate is best used when there are variables that cannot be predicted with adequate certainty, when no reasonably fair alternative method can be determined, when you are not willing to accept any risk, or when court approval is required and the court is accustomed only to hourly fee billing.

The advantages of the hourly rate pricing method include:

- It is familiar to both law firms and clients.
- Rates can be set, quoted, and compared by clients.
- The client pays only for time expended—a subjective judgment of value is not required.
- Time-keeping systems are in place and automatic.
- The risk is placed on the client; the lawyer bears only the risk of nonpayment.

Some disadvantages of hourly pricing include:

- An hourly rate discourages efficiency.
- Clients are frequently surprised by the bill because it is difficult for them to know in advance what the total charges will be.
- The client accepts all the risk, including lawyer inefficiency.
- It promotes client resistance to the perceived high cost of legal services.
- The fee may have little relationship to the value of the services to the client.
- The lawyer is not compensated for results in high-value or high-responsibility cases.
- It frequently does not recognize extraordinary or emergency services.
- It puts a cap on gross income based on the number of billable hours and the rates charged.
- It does not promote efficiency or better ways to provide legal services at a reasonable cost to clients.

Blended Hourly Rate

A modification to the normal hourly rate is the blended hourly rate, in which the client is charged one fee per hour irrespective of who in the firm works on the matter. The partner, whose hourly rate is substantially higher, will be billed at the blended rate as will the associate, whose hourly fee is normally lower. This is one way to market or promote legal services at an apparently lower hourly rate.

While a law firm would make more money if the client were charged the normal hourly rate of the lawyer, the client may be more comfortable with a blended rate, feeling that the hourly rate being charged is less than the partner's normal rate.

With the blended hourly rate, the law firm will make more money if associates rather than the partners can work on the matter.

The main advantage of the blended rate is that it may encourage more delegation of duties, something that encourages law firm efficiency. The main disadvantage to the client is that there may be a disincentive for a partner or senior associate to work on the matter.

Fixed or Flat Fee

This is a fee that is determined in advance of the engagement of counsel, before the lawyer and the client say yes to the representation. The fee is set and a figure is agreed upon that will not vary no matter how much time you expend or what the result is.

A flat or fixed fee encourages the use of systems, delegation, and technology, to make the work process as streamlined as possible. It had better be if the lawyer wants to make a profit. It is best used for routine services or if you are comfortable accepting the risk if costs exceed the fee.

The main advantages of a fixed fee are that it forces agreement between you and the client, the client knows what the fee will be in advance of the engagement (no surprises at the end), and it is not time-dependent; there is no energy spent in time accounting.

The disadvantages relate to law firm profitability. A fixed fee arrangement will not be profitable if services are performed inefficiently, if the cost of providing the service exceeds the estimated cost, if the work is not clearly defined, or if unforeseen difficulties arise.

Value Pricing

This pricing method attempts to correlate the cost of the legal services rendered with the results obtained.

In a commercial matter, one firm recently agreed to perform services at one-half their normal hourly rate if the result anticipated by the lawyer did not occur and three times the normal hourly rate if the result turned out as expected. By lowering the rate and "participating" in the process, the lawyer was able to demonstrate that (1) he or she believed strongly in the case, (2) he or she was willing to share in the consequences of that belief, and (3) the cost to the client, if the lawyer was wrong, would be substantially less than normal.

One of the difficulties of value pricing is deciding what the value is and who determines it. Frequently, the sequence of events is as follows: An estimate of value is determined by the lawyer, the client disagrees, and the court becomes the arbiter in a second, unrelated action by the lawyer against the client for fees. Value pricing is best used when the lawyer and the client have confidence in each other's fairness, and when the value can be determined by a formula in advance.

The advantages of value pricing are that it rewards efficiency and creativity, it is innovative, and it spreads the risk between the firm and the client.

The disadvantages are several, including:

- It is unfamiliar territory for most lawyers.
- If payment is delayed until the end, when the result is known, cash flow is uneven. Responsibility for advancing the

costs of carrying the legal representation needs to be discussed with the client in advance of representation.
- It may be unprofitable if the law firm is inefficient or spends more time than anticipated.
- The risk is spread between lawyer and client (this can be an advantage or disadvantage, depending on which side of the fence you are standing on).
- It does not encourage lawyers to monitor their costs.

Contingent or Percentage Fee

Another version of value pricing is the contingent or percentage fee, where the amount of the fee is based on the value of the recovery for the client, usually a percentage of a favorable result. It is typically used in personal injury, collection, and related types of cases.

Contingent or percentage fees are best used when the client cannot afford legal representation for an interesting or lucrative matter, or when the lawyer is skilled at analyzing and screening cases so that there is a high likelihood of success.

The advantages of contingent or percentage fees are:

- The client pays only in the event of a favorable result.
- It can be lucrative for the lawyer or firm because it is not time dependent, and it encourages efficiency by the lawyer and firm.

The disadvantages are:

- The law firm assumes the risk of providing services without being paid.
- Expenses, usually advanced by the law firm, may not be recovered if the result is other than as expected.
- There is a possible conflict of interest between client and lawyer as to whether and when a matter should be settled or otherwise resolved.
- There may be uneven cash flow, since it is more difficult, though not impossible, to estimate the amount and the timing of money received.
- Statutes in different jurisdictions may limit the contingency percentage recoverable by lawyers in certain matters.

Premium Pricing

This is a form of value pricing or billing where an hourly or other method is used as a base, and, dependent on the result, a premium or added value is charged. Some firms, particularly in complex or high-dollar-value cases, feel justified in assessing such a premium when a particularly good outcome is achieved.

Premium pricing may limit the number of clients who can afford a higher rate, but if the marketplace perceives that you are worthy of it, you may be able to command it.

Sometimes, although rarely, you can assure the client that because of your expertise, the number of hours will be reduced significantly, keeping the total cost at a level comparable to the cost of a less-efficient lawyer who would charge a lower hourly rate.

This method has the same advantages and disadvantages as value pricing except that the law firm will be paid a minimum fee even in the event of a "bad" or unexpected result.

Retainer

This method sets up a fixed-fee-per-time cycle (frequently monthly) for a designated time period (frequently one year). It is sometimes used as a one-time payment to guarantee the availability of the lawyer or firm at a future date. At other times, the retainer is used as a deposit against future services. When an hourly fee is used, the retainer acts as a minimum billing per month.

The advantages of the retainer are that there is the security of knowing the amount and timing of cash flow into the firm, the client is not paying by the hour, and it may be a marketing opportunity for work not covered by the arrangement. For example, clients on retainer frequently bring in additional work for which the lawyer might be entitled to extra billing (depending on the limitations in the retainer agreement).

The disadvantage is mainly that the client may request more services than the retainer fee would warrant if the fee were computed by the hour. If the retainer is a minimum fee to guarantee availability, then there is no disadvantage.

THE USE OF NON-LAWYERS

The use of non-lawyers can be a factor in your pricing strategies. Here is a quick look at the financial impact of using lower-cost paralegals and charging the standard or blended fee of the office:

Billing Person	Cost Based on Hourly Rate	Blended Fee	Profit or Loss
Partner	$175	$150	($25)
Associate	90	150	60
Legal Assistant	50	150	100

The impact of these economics may be even more dramatic in a contingency matter. You can reduce the cost of handling the matter by delegating as much of the work as is reasonably practical to legal assistants. This will allow more time for the lawyer either to do other work that will produce higher total revenue for the firm or, if there is insufficient work for the lawyer, to do marketing to improve the total caseload and revenue for the firm.

Another reason for delegating as much work as possible is that it makes for greater efficiency in the firm. *The lawyer should do only: lawyering and marketing.* That is the most efficient use of his or her time. To do anything else is wasteful and inefficient.

If you charge varying fees for the lawyer and the legal assistant, the firm still benefits from the use of legal assistants (where there is enough work to keep the lawyer busy).

Here are two examples of the effect that using legal assistants has on firm billings:

Example A:

Assume that a typical firm involvement in a client matter would be the following:

10 lawyer hours at $100 =	$1,000
4 legal assistant hours at $40 =	160
Amount of bill	$1,160

Example B:

Assume one variation of the above that allows the lawyer to reduce direct involvement and raise his or her hourly rate. Even if more time is required by the assistant, the cost to the client normally would be the same or less than above:

4 lawyer hours at $150 =	$ 600
14 legal assistant hours at $40 =	560
Amount of bill	$1,160

While one can play with the numbers in the example above in order to achieve a particular result, the principle remains accurate in practice, i.e., that delegating work to the lowest economic level capable of performing the task will result in the greatest revenue and net profits to the firm.

Here is another way of looking at this. If the lawyer is required to dedicate 10 hours to each file, he or she can then handle only 180 files per year (based on 1,800 billable hours per year). If the lawyer can reduce the file time to 4 hours, then the same lawyer can handle 450 files annually. If the lawyer is on contingency, you should be able to see the greater opportunity for increased revenue. If the lawyer is billing based on hourly rates, and can now demand higher hourly rates, the total revenue increases both because of the hourly rate is higher for the lawyer and because more cases are being handled (with the help of the legal assistant).

PRICE SENSITIVITY AND RAISING RATES

To the average client, there is little price sensitivity in choosing a lawyer. That is, the choice is made not because of the fee being charged, but because of other factors such as ability. Usually, the client is in your office because of a referral from a trusted source. Only if the fee difference is very significant (e.g., $50 per hour or more) will the client pause to reflect.

Because of this lack of sensitivity, you can raise hourly rates to new clients by $10 to $15 per hour without fear of client resistance. Usually the same will be true of existing clients. The problem here is that written notice must be given to existing clients before increasing the billing rates, and such a notice will probably cause the client to be aggravated, if not irate, considering the belt-tightening that many clients are experiencing.

Therefore, a better approach might be to increase the rates for new clients and, if you continue to be busy, increase the rates on *new* matters for existing clients. Keep existing rates for present matters until they are concluded.

For ongoing retainers, consider the benefit of regular payments from existing retainer clients—they should be entitled to the benefit of being the last to have their rates increased.

Based on the rule that increased demand can lead to increased fees, the busier you are, the easier it is to raise your hourly rate or increase the fixed fee for any task.

Ultimately, it is the client's (buyer's) perception of value that determines whether the price is reasonable for the service provided. The value of your service is determined by the client.

Price is the marketplace's barometer for telling you how it values your service. Price also determines your profitability. The extent to which you make a profit depends on how much of what you get for your service is above your costs of providing that service.

Over the years, the pricing strategies for lawyers have changed. The time-and-billing-rates (hourly) method of pricing for legal services came into vogue in the early 1900s at the time when manufacturing facilities became enamored with time and motion studies to improve the efficiency of the production line.

Knowing the amount of time spent on each legal file could help determine whether that particular matter was profitable for the law firm. If it was profitable, then could the approach be replicated for the next matter to earn even more money? Or if it was not profitable, could ways be found to improve the efficiency of the law firm's representation the next time around?

There is a seductive simplicity to the hourly fee that causes both clients and lawyers to accept its faults and disadvantages.

You should continue to keep time records even if alternative billing methods are used. The original purpose of such records—knowing whether a profit is made on each file—can be accomplished only if accurate time records are kept.

Because clients are increasingly more sophisticated and because of greater competitive pressures, alternative pricing measures are becoming more prevalent.

We seem to have come full circle. From the fixed fees based on the task or the alternative methods based on results in the 1800s, to the hourly rates of the 1900s, we are now swinging back to the alternative fee methods highlighted in this chapter.

Today, consumers once again seem to want (1) the assurance of knowing the maximum they will have to pay for legal services, and (2) the lowest possible price for those services that they absolutely must have.

An important lesson that many lawyers have learned only recently is the need for greater understanding of the client's needs and appreciation of the client's perceptions of the legal services being offered and delivered. The client is the customer, and the client ultimately determines how legal services are priced.

NOTES

1. This concept is more fully explained by Wesley P. Hackett, Jr., an attorney in East Lansing, MI, in his article, "How to Open and Run a Law Office," published by the General Practice Section, American Bar Association, 1984. Use of his material in this segment of the chapter is with the permission of Mr. Hackett.

2. Wes Hackett has placed several years of his financial statements on computer. He has calculated the overhead costs annually and has confirmed that the variance is small between one year and the next. If the firm grows dramatically by adding lawyers or significant administrative staff, this statement will be modified accordingly. One would expect, however, that such growth will produce sufficient revenue to overcome the added overhead costs incurred.

3. Harris Morgan discusses one formula approach in his article "Value Billing: Fifth Approach," appearing in *Beyond the Billable Hour, An Anthology of Alternative Billing Methods*, Richard C. Reed, ed. Published by the Section of Law Practice Management, American Bar Association, 1989.

4. See, e.g., *Beyond the Billable Hour*, ibid.

CHAPTER 8
The Billing Process

If there's anyone listening to whom I owe money, I'm prepared to forget it if you are.

Errol Flynn

Chapter Checklist
- Clients and the Billing Process
- Who Should Do the Billing?
- What Should Bills Look Like and Contain?
- When Should Bills Be Prepared?
- When Should Bills Be Sent?
- Responses From Clients

Pricing refers to the fee or amount of compensation you initially ask for, and *billing* refers to the actual amount charged for the service rendered. It is the total compensation, including all hourly rates, expenses, markups, etc. But there is much more to billing than that. The billing process is important for two reasons, one obvious and one not.

First, you cannot get paid until you bill. The average national accounts receivable cycle for lawyers' services is 4.3 months. What this means is that it will take, on average, about four and one-half months from the date any bill is received by the client for you to receive the funds. Therefore, any expediting on your part in getting the bills out will assure that this time lag is kept to a minimum. Another less obvious function of a billing statement is that it serves as an important marketing tool if used correctly. Since marketing describes how you relate to and communicate with clients, then the billing process is a natural channel for marketing. It is part of the ongoing, two-way communication process between you and the client, and it is one of the easiest ways to reach existing clients and let them know that you are doing a good job for them.

It is very important to continue marketing to existing clients. Marketing to your current clients is both more effective and less expensive than marketing to prospective or new clients. The "80/20" rule of thumb puts this idea into perspective: On average, 80 percent of your business comes from 20 percent of your existing clients. And your billing statement is one of the easiest ways to reach those existing clients.

With effective billing communication, there is a greater likelihood of "bonding" with clients. "Bonding" is the relationship that develops when you care about clients, and they know it. You connect with clients on a personal level by understanding their true needs and problems and by delivering more than they expect. Complete billing statements let clients know that you are working hard for their interests and that you care.

CLIENTS AND THE BILLING PROCESS

It is important for the client to understand the billing process. Explain it to the client in the initial meeting, or at the time the engagement is being negotiated.

The billing process should then be explained again, in writing, in the letter of engagement. In most jurisdictions it is required that the letter of engagement be in writing.

Ask the client what style or format of billing he or she prefers. This is particularly important for corporate clients. For example, the Corporate Counsel may require the billing statement to be in a particular format to enable the accounting department to process your bill.

WHO SHOULD DO THE BILLING?

The lawyer responsible to the client should do the billing. That lawyer should review and revise, if necessary, all time records of other lawyers and staff members who work on the client's matter.

Even if some records are computerized, billing should not be a mechanical process; much subjective analysis should go into the preparation of billing statements.

Bills can be "written down"—or written off—at the discretion of the billing lawyer if the work done for the client cannot be justified either because of inefficiencies in the process of preparation, learning curves that the client should not pay for, or for client goodwill.

WHAT SHOULD BILLS LOOK LIKE AND CONTAIN?

The actual appearance of the billing statement is a personal matter. There are many quality formats in use today; only the imagination of the lawyer limits the statement's appearance. Obviously, the statement should be dignified and in keeping with the tone of the office and the type of practice.

Standard computer billing programs limit the aesthetic possibilities. If the format of a computer program is not appropriate for your practice, or does not project the image you want to convey to your clients, find a computer consultant to modify and customize the program for you.

If modifying a standard computer program is impractical or not economically feasible, combine original typing with the information gathered from the computer. While you may be duplicating efforts to some extent, you will save time and money, and you can produce the statement format of your choice.

Since the billing statement is a prime marketing tool, it can and should communicate in the most tangible manner possible (other than copies of documents received and sent from your office) what you have done during the month to justify asking for the fee that is in the statement.

The contents of the billing statement should be complete enough to describe the work done so that clients have an appreciation of the effort expended on their behalf.

Billing statements should be accurate. Clients do not like sloppiness from their lawyers; it undermines the client's confidence in the lawyer.

There are three basic types of bills: a simple statement, a time breakout of activities with brief descriptions, and a narrative. The simple statement (see Figure 8.1) merely states that the client owes a certain amount for legal services. There is no description and no detail. The brief description version (see Figure 8.2) lists what actions were taken, when, and how much time they took to complete. The most complete format is the complete narrative description (see Figure 8.3).

There is no question that, from a marketing point of view, a narrative and descriptive billing statement will serve you much better than either of the other two styles. It details your accomplishments, it is action-oriented (use sentences beginning with verbs), it provides a monthly recap of your activities, and it is complete. A narrative bill communicates to the clients that you have taken the time to tell them how hard you have been working for them. Clients appreciate this kind of effort in communication.

Do not forget, it is not the amount of the bill that is important, it is the client's perception of the value received. And the more the client understands the extent to which you are going to solve his or her problems, the more he or she will value your service.

WHEN SHOULD THE BILLS BE PREPARED?

First, time records should be prepared as the work is done. Studies have shown that if time passes between when the work is done and when it is noted, a certain percentage of the time worked never gets recorded. The amount of such lost time can amount to one-half to one hour per day.

Part II: *Techniques for Survival and Growth*

FIGURE 8.1   **Simple Statement**

> January 31, 1993
>
> TO: _____
>
> STATEMENT FOR LEGAL SERVICES
>
> Balance due per previous statement.......................... $
> Less: Received on account .... $
> Balance due:... —0—
>
> Retainer due on February 1, 1993, per agreement
> in connection with legal services rendered.
>
> .... $
>
> Balance due .... $
>
> Thank you for the opportunity to serve you.
>
> Sincerely yours,
>
> Jane Lawyer

Losing one hour per day, multiplied by a billing rate of $100 per hour, equals $500 per week, or $26,000 per year in gross billings lost!

Time records should be gathered regularly, preferably on a daily basis. By reviewing these records at the end of the day, you will have the greatest chance of remembering work that may have slipped through the cracks.

Also, daily time record reviews give you a chance to monitor your progress in achieving your billable-hours-per-day planning goals. And by reviewing a summary of your time records at the end of each week, you will reinforce your success in reaching your billable hours goal or determine the reason(s) for failing to achieve them. This may also point out any inadequacies in your marketing efforts to bring in additional work.

To allow enough time in preparing billing statements, you must determine how much time your office requires to collate and record all unrecorded time records at the end of the cycle.

Chapter 8: The Billing Process

FIGURE 8.2   Time Breakout of Activities with Brief Descriptions

```
                    _____
                    _____
                    _____

                                        PAGE         1
                                        INV#    5-041272
                                        DATE     6/25/93

TO: _____
    _____
    _____
```

RE: 1031 EXCHANGE TAX MATTERS
_____

FOR PROFESSIONAL SERVICES THROUGH MAY 31, 1993:

5/06/93   TELEPHONE CONFERENCE WITH REALTY ATTORNEY RE ESCROW INSTRUCTIONS.

REVIEW ESCROW INSTRUCTIONS AND CHANGES IN FINAL SECTION 1031 DEFERRED EXCHANGE REGULATIONS.

CONFERENCE WITH MR. XXXXXXX RE ESCROW INSTRUCTIONS.

5/15/93   REVIEW PROPOSED EXCHANGE AGREEMENT; ANALYZE SECTION 1031 FINAL REGULATIONS AND REVISE AGREEMENT.

TELEPHONE CONFERENCE WITH XXXXXXX RE TAX COMMENTS ON EXCHANGE AGREEMENT.

5/16/93   ANALYZE TAX ISSUES PRESENTED BY FACTS OUTSIDE EXCHANGE AGREEMENT.

5/22/93   TELEPHONE CONFERENCE WITH MESSRS. XXXXXXX AND XXXX RE EXCHANGE AGREEMENT REVISIONS.

5/23/93   DRAFT SECURITY AGREEMENT PROVISIONS, ESCROW INSTRUCTIONS AND SECURITY AGREEMENTS.

5/28/93   REVISION OF SECURITY AGREEMENT PROVISIONS.

5/29/93   TELEPHONE CONFERENCE WITH MR. XXXXXXX RE SECURITY AGREEMENT: LEGAL RESEARCH RE AGENCY ISSUE.

TOTAL SERVICES	10.00	$2650.00
$- 10.00 \times 265.00 = 2650.00$		

5/31/93   TELECOPY CHARGES   20.00
          DUPLICATION EXPENSES   7.80
                              TOTAL EXPENSES $27.80
                              TOTAL THIS INVOICE $2677.00

FIGURE 8.3 **Narrative Bill**

August 23, 1993

TO: _____

STATEMENT FOR LEGAL SERVICES RENDERED

11/15/92
Telephone conference with Jane Smith, C.P.A.; discussed the importance of concluding the settlement negotiations by December 31st and ramifications to both parties if the previously mutually acceptable dates were not met.

11/18/92
Telephone conference with opposing counsel; discussed spousal support and the tax consequences to each party of various amounts suggested on behalf of both parties; further discussed child visitation and the needs of the children to feel settled in one base. Issues still remain to be resolved, but progess appears to have been made.

11/25/92
Court appearance on motion to modify earlier Court Order in which spousal support had been set; Court granted our motion for reduction and encouraged the parties to continue negotiations for full settlement of all remaining issues.

15 hours @ $200 per hour...................... $3,000
Balance due $3,000

If time records are recorded daily, then this element will require very little time. Print or tally all time records by client and matter. Prepare and print a "prebill" or draft of the billing statement for each client. Review the prebills or billing statements and make changes as may be appropriate. Revise the prebills or drafts of the billing statements and print the final billing statements.

WHEN SHOULD THE BILLS BE SENT?

Billing statements should be mailed so that they reach the client on or before the first day of the month. Clients normally process the bills they have received in the first few days of the month.

Chapter 8: The Billing Process

While this does not guarantee payment of your bill in the current month—payment depends on the client's cash flow and many other factors—prompt receipt does guarantee that your billing statement will be considered at the front of the line.

All statements received after about the fifth of the month are usually considered for payment in the following month. This delay adds thirty days to what would have been the normal account receivable for the client. (TIP: Send a self-addressed, stamped envelope with the bill; it encourages the client to send the payment that much quicker.)

RESPONSES FROM CLIENTS

This is the second part of the two-way communication process. Each alternative response from the client is telling you something, if you only take the time to listen.

The response you expect, of course, is payment for the billing amount, which probably means that the client is satisfied with your work. But you can also learn something if there is no check in the mail.

You may fail to receive payment because (1) the client is unhappy with the size of the bill or unhappy with the quality of the work performed; (2) the client did not ask for or expect the work you performed; or (3) the client simply cannot—or does not want to—pay the bill.

Since you cannot know which of these three reasons is the one responsible for the silence from the client, it is at this point that you need to investigate further (for a more complete description of what is called the "Dial-and-Smile" technique, see chapter 9). Ask questions to probe and find out exactly what the problem is.

When you do not get paid, there is obviously something wrong, and failing to listen to clear signals from the client will only cause further problems for you. After all, do you want to continue working for a client who does not want the work in progress, does not think the work is adequate, or cannot continue to pay for it? Legal work should become *pro bono* only at the discretion of the lawyer, not at the discretion of the client.

CHAPTER 9
Credit and Collections

The urbane activity with which a man receives money is really marvellous, considering that we so earnestly believe money to be the root of all earthly ills, and that on no account can a monied man enter heaven. Ah! How we cheerfully consign ourselves to perdition!

Herman Melville
Moby Dick, 1851

Chapter Checklist
Giving Credit Where It Is Due
Setting Your Credit Policy
Collecting Your Money
Steps to Increasing Your Collections

Credit and collections are two intertwining aspects—Phase 1 and 2—of the same subject: receiving the cash that is owed you for the services that you provide. First, you extend credit to clients as a good-faith gesture with the expectation that you will be paid at a specific time in the future. Then after you have performed the work, you move into phase two: actually collecting that money. Let's look more closely at these complementary concepts.

GIVING CREDIT WHERE IT IS DUE

When the economy is tight, more small service companies, including law firms, try to reel in cash. The problem is, your clients are conserving their cash, too. And that means they are taking advantage of credit terms by paying as slowly, or as late, as possible. Although you do not want to discourage sales by denying credit altogether, it is important to establish a formal credit policy that spells out effective, but fair, credit terms.

The process of establishing or revising credit policies can be unpleasant for many. The thought of laying down the law with customers smacks of negativity, leading many law firm owners to avoid the task altogether. But now is the time to overcome that discomfort so that your firm can maximize income and minimize bad debts.

In reality, conscientious customers will view your credit policy in a positive light. Your willingness and ability to extend credit reflects stability and a long-term commitment to the marketplace. These attributes are valuable to potential customers, who must invest time and money in establishing a relationship with your company. The credit policy lets them know that you are committed to sound business practices and that you plan to be there to meet their future needs.

SETTING YOUR CREDIT POLICY

Approve Clients

The first thing you have to do is approve clients for credit. By spending a small amount of time up front evaluating customers' creditworthiness, you will save a lot of time and money down the road trying to collect bad debts or "dodging the deadbeats."

Check clients' credit history by devising *and using* a credit-approval form designed to capture basic information about any company or individual applying for credit. Ask for: name, address, federal ID number (if a corporation) or social security number (if an individual), driver's license number, business and residence addresses, three trade and personal references plus bank references. Information about loan balances, repayment performance, and the banker's general impression of the customer's business are invaluable in evaluating a client's credit-worthiness. You can also check customers through LEXIS/NEXIS, Dun & Bradstreet, the National Association of Credit Managers, industry trade reports, and credit-rating services such as TRW.

Determine Credit Limits

Determine clients' credit limits in advance and stick to them unless, after *careful* review, there is cause to change the limit. Failure to set the limit in advance will place you in an auction-type, feverish frenzy when the question arises in the midst of performing some sensitive task for the client—a time when either you will not want to walk away from the work or when the court will not permit you to withdraw. Involuntary servitude begins with a failure to set appropriate credit limits.

Set Interest Rates

While it may be helpful to set interest rates for the outstanding balance owing on a bill, the fact remains that if a client fails to pay the amount billed, he or she is unlikely to be able to pay the interest either. Remember that each jurisdiction has different maximum interest rates that you are legally entitled to collect. Frequently, rates also differ based on the status of the client, whether individual or corporate.

Chapter 9: Credit and Collections

The best solution is to receive payment of bills as and when they become due. Avoid using credit policy as a sales tool. You may be tempted to extend credit when business is slow to get more customers to buy your services, but you will be sorry when they cannot pay the bills.

COLLECTING YOUR MONEY

In the best of all possible worlds, soon after you have sent out a bill you will receive an envelope in the mail that contains a check for payment in full. However, since most of us do not live in this perfect world, chances are that you may not receive a check for payment in full. In fact, you may not receive a check at all.

Law firm economics in general are in a state of flux, and the changes are being felt by all lawyers, at large and small firms alike. And late payment or nonpayment of bills is a direct result of tough economic times when everyone is trying to hold on to their money as long as possible.

Are collections really that important? You bet! Uncollected billings that are never seen again—the worst case scenario—represent monies that should have gone into your pockets, but are now a lost cause because all hope of collecting them has gone. They are revenues that now must be offset by more work.

It is important to understand the negative impact that uncollected revenue has on your firm. The amount of new collected bullings required to offset every dollar lost in uncollected billings depends upon your gross margin.

Gross margin is the relationship between funds available for distribution to lawyers (which is what is left over when operating expenses are subtracted from revenues) and total revenues received. It is usually expressed as a percentage (distribution to total revenue). It is one way of seeing how efficient the firm is at distributing "profits" to lawyers. The higher the percentage, the higher the proportion of the firm's revenues that go to the lawyers as salaries or draws.

Let's say that your gross margin is 10 percent. Then you would have to collect $5,000 in new billings to offset $500 in uncollected billings. If your gross margin is 35 percent, you would need to collect $1,429 to offset a $500 loss.

Since uncollected billings mean that you are working for free, your goal is to have them approach zero.

STEPS TO INCREASING YOUR COLLECTIONS

One question that lawyers frequently have is: "We have some difficult clients. How can we collect our accounts receivable? The accounts receivable are higher than they have been at any time in

93

the history of our firm, and they need to be collected now! How do we do it?"

First, let's define "difficult." Usually, a difficult client means one or more of the following:

- The client is not doing what the lawyer wants, i.e, paying the bill.
- The client owes a large amount of money.
- The client has owed the bill for an extended period of time.
- The client has ignored the many requests for payment.

Clients may not pay for a variety of reasons. These reasons run the gamut from anger concerning the quality or price of the legal services rendered to the client's inability to pay not only the legal bill but other bills as well. The reason for a client's failure to pay is important; this information should assist you in determining the approach to take for future collection efforts relating to that client. You can steps take to minimize the chances that any particular client will become a "difficult client."

Communicating

Create a manual or monograph itemizing each of the various collection procedures, form letters, and related documents.

Maintain an accurate listing of accounts receivable. It is essential to know what your clients owe, and having this listing of accounts receivable "aged" is how you can spot if and when a payment problem exists. "Aging" means that the amount owed by each client is spread over time by month created. (Refer to the discussion of aging and to Figure 10.1 in the next chapter.)

Age and review the accounts receivable weekly. Determine who the "problem" clients are and gather information about the nature of their problem. Determine a strategy for dealing with the clients and their particular issues. Do not wait long to address and solve each client's issue.

Statements should contain adequate descriptions to tell the client all the work done. The client will then appreciate the value received for the fee being billed.

Analyze your two-way communication process. The statement that you send to the client is your primary communication explaining what was done for him or her during the preceding period of time (hopefully, no more than thirty days since the previous statement) and what the charges are for that service.

Your client also communicates in a number of ways with a variety of messages. Even when you do not think so, the client is communicating with you, loudly and clearly. Many lawyers usually fail to listen, however, because they are "too busy" to hear the client. (See the discussion of the billing process in the previous chapter for more on this.)

"Dial-and-Smile"

Try the *"Dial-and-Smile"*[1] technique. To really make use of the two-way communication process between you and your clients and to find out what the clients are *really* saying if they are not paying their bills, use this procedure.

First, call the client. That is, have someone else at your firm call; never call the client yourself. Hire someone (a part-time accounts receivable clerk from a local college or a retired bookkeeper) to help you collect. The cost of this person will be less than the money received as a result of his or her efforts. Have the person review each file, contact each client as may be necessary, and pursue collection.

The lawyer should not call the client to collect the outstanding amount owed. Successful businesses do not send their salespeople to their customers to collect; that is handled by a separate credit department. If the lawyer contacts the client for payment, the client may be too embarrassed to continue working with the lawyer. Now, not only has the bill not been paid, but the lawyer has lost a client. Worse still, this client will not refer other potential clients because of his/her embarrassment.

Have the caller ask the client whether he or she *received* the statement. If the answer is no, fax, deliver by messenger, or send a copy of the statement to the client immediately. If the answer is yes, ask the next question, which is whether the client *understands* the statement.

If the answer is no, the caller should tell the client that the lawyer will call shortly to answer any questions the client may have. And be sure *you* call the client as soon as possible to clarify any misunderstandings the client may have. If the client does understand the statement, have the caller ask whether there is any problem with the bill. If the answer is yes, get the information about the nature of the problem and deal with the issue appropriately under the circumstances. If the client says, "No, there is no problem with the bill," then ask the next question: "When can we expect to receive payment in our office?" (not "When will the check be mailed?").

Normally, the client will make a commitment for a certain (even if for only a partial) payment. Mark the calendar for that date. Attempt to get a commitment of no further than 10 days out. If the check does not arrive on time, call the client on the very next day and go through the same set of questions. Each set of calls should be approximately 10 days apart. Complete this process several times over a period of not more than six to eight weeks.

After this time, if the bill is not paid, or at least reduced substantially, you must decide whether to continue working for the client or terminate the lawyer-client relationship and, then, whether to sue for fees earned to date but not paid.

Be sure that the client's responses are being noted in the file. This will build a record that no complaint was ever registered by the client and unanswered in the event that you should have to sue the client to collect fees or if the client should, at some future date, bring a case for malpractice.

The caller should always be friendly and smiling on the telephone (hence the term "dial-and-smile"). The caller should, under no circumstances, be accusatory or in any way hostile to the client, even if the client fails to honor one or more commitments for the payment of money due.

Plan for Payment

A payment plan may be suggested if the client does not offer anything concrete or acceptable. One such plan may involve payment on a current basis (essentially, COD) with some additional sum being applied toward the old bill (plus a fair rate of interest). At least, the bill accrued to date will not increase and you will receive additional business.

Discuss compensation in advance. During the first meeting between you and the client, the issue of fees or recoveries must be discussed. This is a crucial step in minimizing collection problems down the road. Clients appreciate not having to raise the issue. It is better for the lawyer to acknowledge that the issue must be dealt with and to obtain an agreement that both parties can accept.

Prepare a written fee/compensation agreement, to be signed by both you and the client. The written agreement should explain all charges to be made and the need for timely payment of each bill by the client. This agreement, and each statement mailed to the client, should have language similar to the following: "If you have any questions concerning this statement, please contact the law firm immediately. If the firm does not hear from you within ten days, you agree that the statement is accurate and valid."

Deposit all checks from clients even if the amount received does not match the amount due per the statement. Make a photocopy of the check. After making the deposit, call the client. After you have played "telephone tag" for several days, ask the client to explain the difference. You will ultimately reconcile the amount paid with the amount due; however, in the meantime, you will have deposited the amount sent to you and continue to receive the benefits of that deposit.

Retainers

In the case of retainers, you should increase the retainer, consistent with market pressures, to the point that a substantial portion of the initial phase(s) of the task to be accomplished will be covered by the retainer. This effectively reduces the risk of bad debt in the case of collection problems.

To the extent allowed by competitive market pressure, you should stay ahead of the client by having a sufficient retainer in the client's trust account to bill against. Indicate in the written fee agreement that a portion of the retainer will be placed in the trust account and will remain there until computation of the final billing for the client. In the interim, monthly statements will be sent to the client and the amount billed must be paid monthly. This "extra" sum improves your assurance of being paid fees as and when billed. It can be compared to a security deposit a tenant delivers to a landlord when renting real property.

Prepare the Client

Do not promise work product sooner than realistically possible after considering the complexity of the matter and the workload of your office. Lawyers must do the work promised in the time promised. If, for any reason, the work cannot be performed in the manner and in the time promised, you need to communicate with the client. The client must be kept informed of the progress of the matter. A friendly, caring secretary or other staff person can effectively convey the message. The client will accept change if told in advance of the due date.

Tell the client what to expect each step of the way. Do not "hype" the client. If possible, include a tentative or expected timetable of events. The client's perception of the legal problem frequently is different from the reality determined by the lawyer. Educate the client. Unless the client has a thorough understanding of the problem, the efforts of the lawyer and the services rendered will not be fully understood or appreciated. Failed expectations cause many problems. And unpaid lawyer bills tend to stay that way—unpaid.

The Billing Cycle

Change your billing cycle. Bill one-fourth of the alphabet each week. In this manner, you will receive money from clients on a regular basis, probably weekly, rather than once per month.

Shorten your billing cycle. If you remain on the monthly billing cycle, be sure your clients receive your statements on or before the first day of the following month. To do this, your billing cycle must end on or about the 25th of the month.

The theory is that most people pay their bills on or about the first of the month. If a statement reaches the client after this time, the statement is normally placed in the pile of bills to be paid in the following cycle. That means a delay for payment of your statement for as much as 75 days. The first 30 days you are doing the work; the second 30 days is the missed payment cycle of the client; then it takes at least 15 days for the client to write and mail the check and for the mail to deliver the check to you. If the client delays payment even further, the time extends beyond 75 days.

Thus, anything you can do to shorten the cycle will be that much better for you.

Use remittance envelopes, pre-addressed and stamped, and mail them with your statements. This saves the client time and effort in mailing your payment and, frequently, saves at least one day in your receiving payment.

Time Your Statements

Send statements after a particularly beneficial psychological event even if it is somewhat before or beyond the normal billing date. For example, after you have won a motion in court, prepared a draft of an important contract with which your client is pleased, or closed the negotiation on a deal that favors your client, send a billing of services rendered to date. This will place the client on the peak of the "client satisfaction curve," the time of least resistance for payment of fees. Later, the client will invariably forget how important you were to the favorable result and wonder why the bill is so high. Once the client is in that state of mind, the statement for services will sit unpaid until some future date.

Last Resorts

Stop work! If the client does not participate in the process by keeping a promise to pay as billed, do not continue to work for the client. Either notify the client or, in certain circumstances, make an appropriate motion before the court to be removed from the case.

Sue! Some statistics show that the lawyer-creditor is successful in more than 95 percent of litigation against a client-debtor. Malpractice cross-complaints or counterclaims are not automatic responses. Of course, when litigation occurs between a lawyer and client, it is obvious that there will be no future relationship between the two—an automatic loss of future business.

Collecting unpaid fees is never pleasant. But, by following the suggestions above, you can make the task easier. And, most important, the client will be more satisfied, will believe that he or she is receiving legal services of the highest quality, and will be a walking advertisement for you.

NOTE

1. This effective "dial-and-smile" technique was first suggested to me by Eric Shaw, president of New York Credit, based in Marina Del Rey, California.

CHAPTER 10
Methods of Determining Revenue

Remember that money is of a prolific generating nature. Money can beget money, and its offspring can beget more.
Benjamin Franklin
in a letter to "My Friend, A.B.," 1748

Chapter Checklist **Revenue Pattern Analysis**
Turnover Ratio
Aging Analysis
Payment Pattern Analysis

In chapter 5, you learned that revenues are sources of cash to the firm; they increase the cash available. A big question that many lawyers have is, "How can I accurately determine how much revenue to forecast in my cash flow plan?" In that same chapter I gave an example of the most obvious way to do this: Looking at your historical records, take what you received last year and, thinking about what will happen in the next year, simply adjust the revenue expectations up or down accordingly. These expectations are based on a number of factors, including new cases, contracts, or retainers; anticipated engagements, based on affirmative or positive responses to your marketing efforts; and expectations of competitive pressures within the legal profession in your particular area of practice.

To be accurate in these projections (and you can be) requires that you know your clients well enough to anticipate their needs. As an aside, this close relationship also will assure that you are the lawyer from whom the clients will seek all their legal needs.

But, for the more arithmetic-oriented person, there are other mechanisms for projecting the revenues to be expected and received in the future. Four of them are Revenue Pattern Analysis, Turnover Ratio, Aging Analysis, and Payment Pattern Analysis.

REVENUE PATTERN ANALYSIS

First, by looking at the financial information that you have gathered, prepare a *year-by-year* schedule indicating the revenue you

Part II: Techniques for Survival and Growth

received in previous years. Now start looking to see if there are any apparent patterns that stand out.

The patterns may be as simple as the following examples:

- You received at least 10 percent more revenue each year for the last three years.
- Your flow of annual revenue fluctuated up or down in proportion to the amount of time and energy you spent in bar association activities.
- There was no apparent pattern for the growth (or decline) of your revenue.

Next, by looking at the same information, prepare a schedule that shows the revenue you received on a *monthly* basis within each of the previous years. Again, look for patterns.

For example, say you receive a similar proportion of your revenue in the second and third quarters of the year (April-May-June and July-August-September), the largest percentage in the first quarter (January-February-March), and the smallest proportion in the last quarter (October-November-December). Your revenue flow has probably fluctuated up or down in relation to the seasonality of your major clients' industry patterns or in proportion to some other identifiable variable. What is that variable?

Take family law as a practice area example. In the month of December, because of the approaching holidays, new court filings will decline considerably, although visitation or custody disputes may actually increase. In agricultural law, the summer months are usually the busiest because of harvests. Almost every practice area has a certain degree of seasonality associated with it, and that will be reflected in your revenues and cash flow.

TURNOVER RATIO

Where no apparent revenue pattern is observed, try some simple accounting and arithmetic techniques that will help guide your decision-making process.

The typical accounting measure, frequently used by accountants and bankers to determine whether there is a problem in the collection of accounts receivable, is the "turnover ratio" or "average days billings outstanding." This ratio is determined by the following formula:

Turnover ratio = Accounts receivable balance divided by the result of last month's billings divided by the number of days in the month.

or: $$TR = \frac{\text{Accounts Receivable Balance}}{\text{Last Month's Billings/Days in Month}}$$

Let's follow a hypothetical example. Say you are doing this analysis at the beginning of February, and the accounts receivable balance at the end of the previous quarter (October-Novem-

Chapter 10: Methods of Determining Revenue

ber-December) was $200,000. Taking January's total billings of $75,000 and dividing it by the 31 days in January equals $2,419. Dividing $200,000 by $2,419 equals a turnover ratio of 83 days. This means that your average bill "turns over" every 83 days, or saying it another way, it will take you 83 days on average to collect your bills.

Even more frequently, the formula is stated in annual terms (last year's sales or billings):

$$TR = \frac{\text{Accounts Receivable Balance}}{\text{Annual Billings}/365\,\text{Days}}$$

Following the above example, $200,000 is the accounts receivable balance at the end of the year, annual billings are $900,000, and there are 365 days in the year. Plugging the numbers into the formula gives you a turnover ratio of 81 days.

Unfortunately, and as you can see by our examples, the turnover ratio is normally different depending on which of these two formulas are used. Which is correct? Both are. You decide which is the most appropriate method for your practice.

The turnover ratio will, on average, tell you that you can expect to receive payment for your billings X number of days after the client receives your billing statement. *The national average for law firms, according to one survey, is between 4 and 5 months, or 120 to 150 days.* Implicitly, this should tell you that you need to capitalize your firm with funds sufficient to "carry" your clients for at least six months of billings if you do not want to face serious cash pressures in the interim.

The turnover ratio—whichever formula is used—is an accounting procedure that nonservice businesses have been using for years. There is no reason why law firms cannot make use of this excellent method in helping them project their revenues. Remember, though, this is only a guide and should be tested against your own experience.

AGING ANALYSIS

There is another accounting measure that may be helpful in predicting when you can expect to receive cash. It is called an "aging analysis."

First, review your accounts receivable aging chart or schedule or prepare one if none existed before (see Figures 10.1 and 10.2 and the blank form in Appendix B). A quarterly general ledger can also show this information (see the General Ledger example in Appendix E).

The accounts receivable aging schedule (Figure 10.1) will show how old each client's billing is by how much money that client owes for each period of time (30-day periods are standard). The first column (0–30) represents the first 30 days after the billing cycle (this is typically considered a current bill that is not yet

Part II: Techniques for Survival and Growth

FIGURE 10.1 Sample Accounts Receivable Aging Analysis

Month of: November 1993

Name of client	0–30	31–60	61–90	91–120	121–150	More than 150
A	$5,000	$3,000	$3,000			
B			$6,000	$500		
C			$5,000			
D						$3,000
E				$2,000		
F	$7,500	$5,000				
G	$4,000					
H	$15,000					
TOTAL	$31,500	$8,000	$14,000	$2,500	$–0–	$3,000

due). Each column thereafter represents another 30 days from the original billing-cycle date.

Obviously, the longer the bill is owed or the older the bill is, the less likely it is that you will ever collect it. Therefore, it is important to pay close attention to your accounts receivable aging analysis.

Looked at in another way, Figure 10.2 shows the status of your billings by percentage per period of time. Prepare a schematic as shown in Figure 10.2 (use the blank form in Appendix B), using the monthly totals for each aging period.

This schedule is based on the preceding year, on a quarterly basis. Look at the numbers at the end of each quarter and determine how "old" the receivables were. Fill in the numbers. (See Figure 10.2 for an example.) You could make the presentation even more complete by doing it on a monthly basis, using the information supplied in Figure 10.1 for each of the respective

FIGURE 10.2 Sample Accounts Receivable Aging Schedule by Percentage by Quarter

Days Outstanding	1st Qtr. (Jan–Mar)	2nd Qtr. (Apr–Jun)	3rd Qtr. (Jul–Sep)	4th Qtr. (Oct–Dec)
0–30 days	40%	45%	50%	53%
31–60 days	34%	20%	18%	14%
61–90 days	15%	18%	20%	24%
91–120 days	6%	5%	4%	4%
121–150 days	3%	8%	3%	–0–
151+ days	2%	4%	5%	5%
Total:	100%	100%	100%	100%

months. (Use the blank form for Accounts Receivable Aging by Percentage by Month in Appendix B.) Greater accuracy would be achieved by using as many months as are available, e.g., two to three years.

Trends and patterns can usually be observed by analyzing the schedules above. An average or high and low benchmarks can be determined that will be useful in predicting how much of each month's future billing will be collected in cash.

High growth rates and volatile billings can make these measures less accurate for projections of future revenue, but they are still valid guides when nothing else is available.

PAYMENT PATTERN ANALYSIS

The previous two methods of determining accounts receivable liquidity are usually adequate, but they are not perfect, especially if your practice is growing rapidly or if it has a highly seasonal revenue pattern. An even more accurate way of forecasting when the cash from future billings will be received is called the Payment Pattern Analysis (PPA).[1] My variation of this theory goes like this:

Based on billings in each month, determine for the last year what percentage of the monthly billings were paid in each *succeeding* month. This can be done by percentages of the total billings (see Figure 10.3).

Part II: Techniques for Survival and Growth

FIGURE 10.3   Sample Payment Pattern Analysis (by Averages)

Month of billing	First month after bill	Second month after bill	Third month after bill	Fourth month after bill	Fifth month after bill	Sixth month after bill	More than six months after bill
(Sample % for Jan.)	10%	20%	30%	15%	15%	5%	5%
Jan.	$	$	$	$	$	$	$
(% for Feb.)							
Feb.	$	$	$	$	$	$	$
(% for Mar.)							
Mar.	$	$	$	$	$	$	$
(% for Apr.)							
Apr.	$	$	$	$	$	$	$
(% for May)							
May	$	$	$	$	$	$	$
(% for June)							
Jun.	$	$	$	$	$	$	$
(% for July)							
Jul.	$	$	$	$	$	$	$
(% for Aug.)							
Aug.	$	$	$	$	$	$	$
(% for Sept.)							
Sep.	$	$	$	$	$	$	$
(% for Oct.)							
Oct.	$	$	$	$	$	$	$
(% for Nov.)							
Nov.	$	$	$	$	$	$	$
(% for Dec.)							
Dec.	$	$	$	$	$	$	$
TOTAL	$	$	$	$	$	$	$

You can go through your case file and determine when each client has typically paid the bill. Mr. Smith usually pays in the third month, Mr. Jones in the second, Mr. Johnson in the fifth. The results of this analysis adjusted to the amounts of each client's bills will give you a good basis for filling in the percentages

Chapter 10: Methods of Determining Revenue

in Figure 10.3. This method may be the most informative and complete method of learning current payment patterns. With this information, projections will be far more accurate. However, this method is also more time-consuming and difficult, especially in a high-volume practice. Use the blank form in Appendix F.

A quicker, down-and-dirty way of doing it is to refer to Figure 10.1, the accounts receivable aging listing by client. The "total" at the bottom of each column would be the numerator; the denominator would be the total receivables for the month. Figure the percentage of the total for each period (i.e., 0–30, 31–60, etc.) and simply assume that these amounts *owed* will roughly equal when they were *paid*.

For example, 15 percent of the billings may be owed in the first month (0–30 days) after billing. Then let's say that 20 percent is owed in the second month (31–60 days) after billing. And so on. Once you have all the percentages, you can fill in the appropriate figures month by month in Figure 10.3 (use the blank form in Appendix F).

After you fill in Figure 10.3, based on your firm's past experience, you may notice the percentages change in certain months. For example, the percentage of collections may be lower in the months of April, August, and December. If this is the case for you, the reason may reflect a slowing down of bill paying around tax time (April) and also around the winter holiday (December). The August fluctuations may result from vacation time for you or your clients in the earlier months of June or July. While collections from previous bills should hold steady, the billing amounts during this time are likely to go down since some people are not there to do the work (either in your office or in your client's accounts payable department). Consequently, the lower amount of payments from that low-billing period will not show up until several months later.

This analysis would—and should—also adjust for any other factors that are specific to your practice, region, or situation.

It is even more accurate and revealing if you perform the same analysis on a client-by-client basis. To do this, refer to the ledger sheet maintained by the firm for each respective client.

NOTE

1. Payment pattern analysis was first described by Professor Bernell K. Stone in "The Payment Pattern Model to Forecasting and Control of Accounts Receivable," *Financial Management* (Autumn 1976), pp. 65–82. Professor Stone stated that if the pattern of the source event (billings) can be predicted, then the pattern of the event's cash flow can be accurately predicted. This pattern can best be used to monitor the payment pattern of individual clients. In fact, when the lawyer has several major clients, the analysis can most effectively be applied to the individual clients to determine when cash payment can be expected.

CHAPTER 11
Banks and Loans

You want 21 percent risk-free? Pay off your credit cards.
Andrew Tobias
quoted in American Way magazine
November, 1982

Chapter Checklist   Financial Needs
What About a Loan?
Types of Loans
Selecting a Banker
Getting to Know the Banker
Understanding the Bank's Loan Requirements
Documents the Bank Wants to See
Additional Information to Discuss with the Bank

FINANCIAL NEEDS

Law, as any other business, requires money to operate, and sometimes, money is in short supply. The reasons for that and the kinds of money or cash that may be needed can be many. Here are some examples:

Seed money. This is the initial money you need to get you going in planning a new business. Consider it "earnest money." It is the financial outlay that proves you are serious about this endeavor.

Start-up capital. This is what pays for the equipment and other initial expenses of getting the firm underway. This is the money that really gets the firm going, but barely. Vendor terms (buying on credit) are also considered a form of start-up money.

Working capital. Working capital is money used to finance accounts receivable and operating expenses. These are the funds that keep you afloat until the cash flow from the business starts flowing in your direction.

Growth capital. These are funds used for expanding sales (and the increase in accounts receivable), purchase of additional equipment to handle larger demand for your services, and adding new people to supplement existing staff. Usually growth is financed from the profits of the firm, but the profits may be too narrow or the growth may be too great to be handled by the existing level of profits.

The next obvious question is, How much money do you need? The key word here is "need," not "want." Think only about what your firm needs to survive; do not—at this point—think about how much you are going to take out for personal pleasure, comfort, or peace of mind.

Here are some factors that determine this financial need:

Sales volume. The greater the billings, the greater the need for cash in the firm. Why? Nationally, the average time between when you bill someone and when you receive the payment is approximately four and one-half months. This means that the greater the billings, the greater the amount of cash needed to hold you through this waiting period. Some firms actually limit their capital needs by limiting their billings. One way to do that is by raising prices; the number of clients will be reduced.

Growth rate. Faster-growing firms require more money; these can be real "money eaters." By increasing your accounts receivable and your workload, you increase the need for more personnel, more office space, etc. And although your clients may take over four months to pay you, your staff, landlord, and outside vendors expect to be paid *now*. Growth must be managed very carefully or the entire "ship" may sink.

Gross margin. Gross margin is what is left over after you subtract operating expenses from revenues. It reflects the degree of "profits" the firm generates that are distributed to the lawyers as salaries or draws. The lower the margin, the greater the need for additional outside funds. The larger the margin, the higher the profits of the firm and the smaller the requirement for additional funding or sources of funds.

Conversion cycle of assets. This is often called "capital turnover," or how often the invested assets of the firm are being returned in revenues. The higher the rate of turnover, the more sales can be produced on the same amount of assets. In professional practices, the net effect of this concept is to understand the cycle of accounts receivable turnover—how soon you can get paid by your clients after you bill them.

Lead times. The longer it takes to get something accomplished (e.g., training an associate to take on more sophisticated matters), the more money is required.

Chapter 11: Banks and Loans

Terms of sale. The more lenient you are in the credit terms you extend clients (see more about this in chapter 9), the more money you will require to stay in business. The sooner you get paid, the sooner you can use your profits (revenue minus costs) to finance your own growth.

The main thing to remember is that you are not in the banking business! When you bill clients, you are extending them credit. The more lenient you are with your credit terms or terms of sale, the greater the risk that you will not be paid. The more you do this, the more you become a lender or a banker to your clients. The American Bar Association recently ruled against lawyers being able to conduct ancillary business activities (NOTE: Rule 5.7 of the ABA Model Rules of Professional Conduct was rescinded in August 1992 on a close vote.) Do not become your client's banker!

WHAT ABOUT A LOAN?

Let's say, for example, that your firm is not collecting on its accounts receivable as quickly as anticipated. This is particularly true in today's business environment when many clients of law firms (small and large) are experiencing sales downturns, causing the clients to stretch out their payments.

Or maybe—and for quite the opposite reason—the firm is growing quickly. During a period of expansion, additional cash is required to finance the hiring of new personnel (including lawyers) and the purchase of new facilities and/or equipment. Unless additional capital is raised from among existing partners, cash must be borrowed in order to meet the cash demands of such growth.

Money can also be in short supply when new equipment is purchased to replace old equipment. For example, when a new computer or telephone system is installed, additional cash funds will be required.

A common denominator in each of these situations is that the cash needs exceed the firm's own cash generation ability. When that happens, the firm must have a source from which to obtain the extra cash that it needs in the form of a loan.

There are several loan sources available. The least expensive is for the partners to advance additional capital to the firm. But, normally, the partners of a small firm do not have extra cash at hand. Therefore, the firm must borrow the additional cash required. Relatives of the lawyers are one source of cash, but lawyers usually avoid this route. Borrowing money from relatives is often viewed by lawyers as unprofessional or as an admission of failure. Under these circumstances, then, it is nice—and sometimes crucial—to have a good relationship with a bank. Banks

Part II: Techniques for Survival and Growth

have the marvelous facility of being able to loan money to deserving borrowers to help them get over the periods when their cash flow is less than expected. Following are some tips, considerations, and important factors that can help in the acquisition of a bank loan.

TYPES OF LOANS

Some banks have set specific guidelines in the granting of loans to lawyers and law firms. These are guidelines used by the typical banking institution:

- *Line of credit or revolving line of credit.* The amount of the loan is dependent on each bank's perception of the total loan package. Some banks limit a loan to three times the monthly expenses, excluding partner draws. In the case of a line of credit, the borrower may borrow and repay at will up to the amount of the "line"; the bank usually prefers that the borrower be "clean" or out of debt for at least 30 days to 90 days each year. The line of credit is then reviewed annually and extended, increased, or terminated as circumstances warrant. In the case of a revolving line of credit, the borrower usually obtains a designated sum of money over a period of time. The revolving line of credit is then converted to a term loan and is repayable over a period of two, three, or five years.
- *Equipment term loan.* The amount of the loan will normally be no more than the depreciable life of the equipment, usually three to five years. Some borrowers may be able to obtain loans for a longer period, but this is usually when the equipment being financed is expected to last longer than equipment typically acquired for use by a law firm.
- *Term loan.* These loans can be as long as seven to ten years for a large law firm and three to five years for a smaller firm. Most such loans involve leasehold improvements and furniture and equipment purchases. Frequently, the term loan is drawn down over a period of six to nine months; the payback period begins within three months of the final draw. The periodic payments may be structured to be equal payments until paid in full or the loan may provide for a balloon payment at the end of the term.

SELECTING A BANKER

Not every lawyer can properly represent every client. So, too, not every bank is appropriate for every lawyer. It is important for lawyers to know the prospective banker; know the types of loans they prefer; know the type of customer base the bank is seeking to build; know the general pricing structure of the bank; and know how flexible the bank will be in seeking new ways of helping the lawyer or firm with its future plans.

Lawyers and law firms are generally attractive customers for banks desiring to grow. Banks believe, and rightly so, that good lawyers have the ability to both stay employed and to accumulate a substantial net worth. Lawyers, aside from being good customers themselves, tend to be opinion leaders in the business community and are viewed by the bank as a rich source of referrals (networking).

Lawyers should look for a bank that gives them the types of services and responsiveness they want. A bank can effectively handle not only the needs of the firm but also personal banking needs as well. For example, banks typically offer the following types of services for law firms:

- Credit arrangements to finance office relocation, leasehold improvements, capital expenditures and capital contributions, and other aspects of firms' cash needs.
- An on-line financial network to facilitate cash management. For example, banks offer the opportunity to set minimum and maximum cash balances in the firm's general account, with "extra" funds being transferred daily to money-market, interest-bearing accounts and cash advances being drawn from a line of credit in the event the general account falls below the minimum.
- An attorneys' investment account (also known as a clients' trust account), which can simplify the management of clients' funds, consolidate record keeping and year-end Internal Revenue Service report preparation.
- Payroll administration, including tax reporting and record keeping.
- Banking services for staff of the firm.
- Short-term investment instruments such as certificates of deposit, business money-market accounts, commercial paper, U.S. government agency repurchase agreements, and other portfolio options.
- Pension plan administration.

Banks offer the following types of services for individuals (both for the lawyers and staffs of law firms):

- Personal loans
- Home mortgages
- Interest-earning deposit accounts
- Discount brokerage
- Custody (trust) services
- Trust and estate services
- Personal financial planning

Part II: Techniques for Survival and Growth

The foregoing list of services is frequently not available all at one bank. However, the larger banks in metropolitan areas do offer all of the foregoing, and more. The needs of the lawyer and the law firm will determine the bank to be selected as the bank of the firm.

GETTING TO KNOW THE BANKER

The borrowing process tends to go faster and smoother when your banker understands your business plan and your business. You can expedite the loan process by meeting with your banker on a regular basis and inviting him or her to your office to see that your business is well managed and that you have good controls in place.

Lawyers need to educate and get to know their banker. The banking relationship must be open, candid, and built on trust. Good bankers are creative people who will find a way to assist a good customer of the bank. The banker can be more creative if he or she fully understands your goals and circumstances. In time, your banker could prove to be a valuable source of information, advice, and possibly even new business.

The old saying was that banks lend money to those who do not need it. Actually, this was never true. It is unreasonable to expect anyone—including a bank—to lend money unless the borrower has something at risk. Thus, a bank will make a loan only if the borrower has a contribution or money in the deal. If you need money, it is hard to get a bank to open its coffers. Thus, it is better to establish the banking relationship and to learn what makes the bank "tick" before funds are needed to avoid a catastrophe (e.g., missing the week's payroll).

Bankers require that borrowers understand their businesses. There are four areas of concern that a banker will definitely quiz you on; the better prepared you are in answering these kinds of questions, the more confident the banker will be.

Financials. Can your business be characterized as a financial success? Why or why not? How does your company compare financially with its competitors? Is your performance solid and consistent? Do you recognize financial shortcomings and understand their origin?

Marketing. Is your marketing approach effective? How do you measure this effectiveness? Do you understand the link between marketing and financial results? Do you manage your marketing resources efficiently?

Management. Is your firm well managed? Does it incorporate a good mix of management skills? Do the managers have quantitative and qualitative problem-solving capabilities? Describe any weaknesses.

Product. Does your product (providing legal services) provide any benefits beyond those of your competitors? Are perceived product benefits accounted for in your pricing? Do your staff members understand product differentiation? Does management know how to price the services, balancing market factors with costs?

UNDERSTANDING THE BANK'S LOAN REQUIREMENTS

Beyond the points raised above, banks make loans based on "The Four Cs": character, capacity, capital, and collateral. The average banker will weight these factors in the decision-making process as follows: character (80 percent), collateral (15 percent), capacity and capital together (5 percent).

- *Character.* The first question asked by the bank is whether the ethics, business practices, and general reputation of the prospective customer/borrower are such that the bank is comfortable. Does the bank want to do business with this lawyer? Without this threshold question being answered in the affirmative, there is no further discussion. The elements of character are honesty, integrity, and ability.
- *Capacity.* The next question is whether the cash flow of the law firm is such as to justify the confidence that the loan carrying costs (interest and related charges) and the principal amount of the loan will be paid back at the appointed time. A cash-flow statement (not just an income or revenue and expenses statement) *must* be submitted to the bank for their consideration.
- *Capital.* The bank wants to know what the funds are being used for. If the loan proceeds will be used to purchase an asset, the bank wants to know how much of the cost of the asset will be purchased by the law firm with assets of the firm, or, in other words, how much equity (or debt-to-equity ratio) the law firm will have in the asset. Banks do not want to be the only party investing in the given asset; they want to know that the law firm has a substantial stake in the purchase. Bankers are willing to take risks, but their risk is that their borrower will not repay the loan. The risk the bankers do not want to take is that their loan to the law firm (or to any borrower) places them in the position of being the only investor in the purchased asset. The risk that the purchase will accomplish the intended objective is or should be on the borrower, not the banker. The banker wants the bank's risk to be limited to the analysis of the law firm's ability to repay the loan even if the ultimate purchase does not work out or does not produce the income expected. If the law firm has an adequate capital base in the investment, the bank is more comfortable in assisting the firm (borrower) in the completion of the purchase.

Part II: Techniques for Survival and Growth

As a side note, it has been said that law firms often need working capital loans. Technically, the advance of funds under a loan does not change working capital. The more correct statement is that the loan is being made to help the law firm meet its liquidity or cash needs. The bank must be assured that there is sufficient equity in the law firm to repay the loan in accordance with the terms of the loan.

- *Collateral.* Despite the bank having been as careful as it can be in its examination and review of the borrower (due diligence), there still may come a time when the loan will go into default. If all else fails, how will the bank's outstanding loan be repaid? The "back door," as some bankers call it, is the value and adequacy of the collateral that was given to the bank to secure the payment of the debt in accordance with the terms of the loan. What type of collateral will be given to secure payment? Is it a house, another piece of real estate, equipment used in the operation of the law firm, a personal guarantee by someone of significant wealth who will be able to honor the guarantee should it be necessary, or some other asset of substantial value?

In law firms that are organized in the partnership format, there is joint and several liability for the bank loan. Therefore, the partner with the greater asset base may want to insist that there be substantial collateral or, alternatively, may want to request that the potential profit should be greater than for the other partner(s) by virtue of the greater exposure to risk.

If the loan is unsecured, the bank has given up the fourth C (collateral). In today's economic environment, this would be very unusual and occur only with the best of the bank's customers.

DOCUMENTS THE BANK WANTS TO SEE

The following documents should be prepared for presentation to the bank in order to enter into a new banking relationship:

- Partnership agreement
- Annual fiscal year-end statements prepared by an accounting firm acceptable to the bank (two to five years)
- In-house quarterly statements after the last year-end statement
- Aged accounts receivable schedule
- Cash-flow projection, sometimes considered to be an annual budget, for the next twenty-four months
- Personal financial statement of net worth of the principals
- Personal tax returns of the principals (two to five years)
- Law firm tax returns (two to five years)

Chapter 11: Banks and Loans

Additional documents such as a business interruption insurance policy and disability and/or life insurance policies may be required. Further, these instruments may have to be assigned to the bank as additional collateral to secure the payment of the loan.

ADDITIONAL INFORMATION TO DISCUSS WITH THE BANK

In addition to furnishing the documents to the bank, be prepared to discuss with the banker the following issues that help complete the picture concerning your law firm's viability and future growth prospects:

- *Financial statements.* Are your statements prepared on an accrual or cash basis? Most statements are prepared on an accrual basis; be sure your banker understands the difference between the two. If the law firm's financial statements are prepared on a cash basis, be sure to submit schedules of liabilities (accounts payable, etc.) and accounts receivable, neither of which will show up on a cash-basis financial statement.
- *Capital adequacy.* How much of the law firm's capital is permanent? What are the pay-out and pay-in policies of the firm?
- *Hidden assets.* Are there any hidden assets of the firm such as a lease that has increased significantly in value? Are there significant billable hours that have not yet been billed? Are there contingency cases that are ripe for settlement or promise to be winners in a forthcoming trial?
- *Billing practices.* What are your billing rates? How do these rates compare with the industry? How frequently are statements delivered to clients? What are the aging, reserve, and write-off policies of the firm? How quickly are receivables collected (turnover rate)?
- *Litigation risk.* Does the firm carry an errors and omissions insurance policy? What are the deductible and premium?
- *Cost controls.* What is the gross profit margin of the firm? Are there any major cost-containment programs in effect? Are there any major cutbacks or expansions planned in the near future?
- *Partner control.* Does any one partner or group of partners control a significant percentage of the firm's business? Does any one partner control the business decisions of the firm?
- *Client base.* What type of client is attracted to the firm? Is the client relationship based on transactions or on relations with the lawyer or law firm? Is the firm focused on one area of practice or is it a diverse practice?
- *Management.* How is the firm governed?
- *Financial strength.* Review ratios of liquidity, leverage, and debt capacity. Review profits per partner and revenue per lawyer.

Part II: Techniques for Survival and Growth

Lawyers should think of the bank as a supplier. Suppliers provide lawyers with the goods and services that allow the law firm to deliver quality legal services. One of these suppliers, for most lawyers, should be the bank. Good banking relationships provide the necessary funds and services to allow a law firm to maintain itself and grow.

CHAPTER 12
Should You Hire an Executive Director?

I am richer than E. E. Harriman. I have all the money I want and he hasn't.

John Muir

Chapter Checklist   **The Executive Director's Job**
A Profit Center for the Firm
Measuring Benefits

Small firms and sole practitioners are spending precious time managing their firms when that time could be better spent lawyering. Hiring a part-time executive director is one way a solo or small firm can better manage the practice, deliver higher-quality legal services, and make more money doing it. Law is a business, and lawyers are asking serious questions about the economics of their practices. One such question is, "How can I better manage my practice?"

The traditional lawyer's team consists of the lawyer, a secretary, and perhaps a paralegal. The team may also have a part-time bookkeeper or accountant. One answer to the question of how to better manage a practice, even a solo practice, is to increase the lawyer's team of players who provide additional expertise. The added team member would be an executive director.

THE EXECUTIVE DIRECTOR'S JOB

An executive director manages the firm. He or she helps the lawyer identify the problem areas of the firm; suggests and creates solutions to the problems; arranges for the personnel to be trained to handle the solutions; and provides follow-up involvement and guidance.

Within this general framework, the specific tasks an executive director performs are many. They are as varied as are lawyers who practice law. These tasks include: facilitating and participat-

Part II: Techniques for Survival and Growth

ing in the process of preparing a business plan; preparing or facilitating the preparation of a marketing plan; preparing or facilitating the preparation of cash-flow projections; collecting accounts receivable; establishing and maintaining good relations with the firm's creditors including, but not limited to, the firm's banker; organizing the office routine; hiring necessary employees as the firm grows or as new personnel are required to replace retiring personnel; facilitating and arranging for the training of employees, both at the staff and professional levels; buying new equipment; creating purchasing procedures for supplies; leasing new facilities; and all the other, myriad details of running a practice as a business.

When discussing the functions of an executive director, most people imagine a full-time, on-site employee. However, all the above tasks can be performed by someone on a part-time basis, either on-site or from the office of the independent contractor. In fact, there is a burgeoning industry of "hands-on" management of the administrative tasks of small law firms and sole practitioners by these independent consultants.

Executive directors should have developed management skills as a result of education and training. They also need good people skills (especially when it comes to interacting with other employees) and good organizational skills. They should also have references from other law firms or other service businesses.

A PROFIT CENTER FOR THE FIRM

In a law practice, the lawyer is the revenue center. The executive director will not produce revenue. However, the executive director will produce—or cause production of—profits. This is accomplished in several ways.

First, the executive director can do tasks, as noted above, that the lawyer would otherwise have to do. If you can turn your attention to doing more lawyering (normally a higher per-hour value than managing), the total revenue will increase and the total profit for the firm will increase. If you do not do more lawyering but, rather, do marketing for the firm, the firm's future will be assured as the marketing produces more business.

Further, the executive director will be sensitive to the costs the firm is incurring for maintenance of the firm's library, health insurance, malpractice (E&O) insurance, and other "big ticket" costs. The executive director, by taking more time than is normally available to the lawyer to focus his or her attention on reducing costs to the firm, can usually cause a reduction of costs or at least "hold the line" on increases that might otherwise occur.

Thus, by reducing costs, by creating efficiencies within the firm, and by allowing the lawyer greater opportunity to do more lawyering, the executive director is a direct contributor to the profit (as contrasted to revenue) of the team.

MEASURING BENEFITS

Most lawyers, especially sole practitioners, concede that they spend ten to twenty hours per week doing what they consider to be management activities. Assuming a billing rate of $100 per hour (a very modest rate, to be sure), the value of the time expended by a lawyer in management activities exceeds $1,500 per week (at, e.g., fifteen hours per week), $6,450 per month, or $78,000 per year. If 50 percent of these management activities were performed by an executive director, resulting in time saved by the lawyer, $39,000 would be "saved"; the actual savings would be less because the firm would incur the cost of the executive director. But the cost of an executive director for seven or eight hours per week would be substantially less than $39,000 per year. (The compensation range is roughly $50 to $100 per hour.) The net difference is profit to the firm.

Therefore, you can measure the prospective gain to be anticipated by hiring an executive director. Of course, if the time presently spent by you on management activities is greater than fifteen hours per week, or if the billing rate exceeds $100 per hour, the net savings will be even greater.

By hiring an executive director, the lawyer, especially the sole practitioner, benefits by having a better-run organization and an organization that will be poised to accept growth and deliver higher-quality legal services to the clients of the firm.

As long as the lawyer is either lawyering in the present or marketing for the future, an executive director would be valuable to the team. The professional approach to managing the firm that is brought by a qualified executive director can be an important, and profit-producing, factor in the delivery of quality legal services.

CHAPTER 13
Playing the Slow Economy Game

During a five-day bicycle race, the racers got the weak end off.
[author unknown]

Chapter Checklist   **Temporary Slowdown**
Downsizing
Demerger
Liquidation

Temporary slowdown, downsizing, demerger, and liquidation—these are all different reactions of law firms to a difficult economic environment. Since law is a business, and business is often equated to the playing fields of sport, football is an appropriate example for the "downturn" strategies of law firms during a slow economy.

Think of your firm as the team and the economy as the opponent. Since the game is never over until the last play, the goal of any team, business, or practice is to stay in the game. There are many strategies that football teams use to position themselves to keep playing and ultimately win. In the legal profession, slowdowns, downsizing, demergers, and even liquidating the firm are not necessarily last, desperate acts, but defensive strategies. They are different ways law firms can play the slow-economy game.

TEMPORARY SLOWDOWN

Early in a football game, if a team is not gaining enough ground in moving the ball down the field, it will usually punt, or kick, the ball to its opponent. The team knows that it will eventually recover the ball, but for now, it is best just to get rid of it and take up a defensive posture. In any game, there are numerous changes in ball possession that are considered a normal part of play.

So, too, with your law firm. There are many peaks and valleys in a firm's life cycle, and solo practitioners and small firms face the valleys of lean times frequently, sometimes more than once each year. Take advantage of the extra time of slow business to work on your marketing efforts to get more clients and/or to get more work from existing clients. Economic valleys are part of professional life. Expansion will occur later when market forces are once again appropriate and when opportunities present themselves.

DOWNSIZING

At the start of each season, a football team has more prospective players than it can use. There is a culling-out period when marginal team members are "cut." These cuts are needed—and, in fact, required by league officials—to bring the team to its most efficient size.

In the medical profession, good doctors first review the least intrusive medical treatment. In the business world, good business persons will review the strategy that will cause the least disruption to the unit. For lawyers, the strategy that will cause the fewest "injuries" to the team is downsizing, or "cutting"—not just eliminating people but saving in other areas too. Here is a list of "cuts"—in order of severity—that the law firm needs to consider to make itself a more efficient team during a slow economy:

- Postpone expansion plans.
- Postpone capital expenditures.
- Postpone bonuses.
- Postpone staff raises.
- Postpone, where possible, equipment and facilities repair and maintenance.
- Reduce partners' income somewhat.
- Lay off some staff.
- Lay off additional staff.
- Lay off some associate lawyers.
- Reduce partners' income further.

But be cautious when downsizing. You must preserve and protect the team and maintain a strong resource base. You still want and expect to win the game. You need to be ready to respond to the economic recovery that is always around the corner.

DEMERGER

In football, teams reorganize by trading players to improve and strengthen their position. Law firms can also reorganize themselves.

In the 1980s, large law firms grew larger by merging or by acquisition. But in a shrinking economy, the opposite can also

Chapter 13: Playing the Slow Economy Game

work. A merged practice can be split up ("demerged") into its premerger units, especially if the separate corporate cultures are still intact.

Alternatively, you may need to cut an area of practice that is not profitable, or you may want to take on a new area of practice that is the sudden rage of the community (elder law, environmental law, bankruptcy practice, etc.).

And finally, segments of a firm or practice or even individual lawyers can break off to form a new boutique or specialty practice.

Another football analogy here is the lateral pass. There has been no loss of yardage, just a delay in reaching the goal line. There is a change in direction, but there is still plenty of time remaining in the game.

LIQUIDATION

When there are only a few minutes remaining on the clock, and the situation looks gloomy, a football team resorts to more-drastic measures in order to win. The "Hail Mary" play is an example. In this last-gasp effort, the quarterback throws a long pass toward the goal line and hopes that one of his teammates will catch it for the winning touchdown. It is a risky maneuver, but at this late stage, there is nothing to lose.

When the law firm's future is in doubt, it may be time to throw the big bomb and consider liquidation. While the firm will cease to exist, it is not the end of life for the individual lawyers. There is still hope in the destruction of the firm. Individual lawyers can join another team (there are, after all, other teams in the league) or create a new firm. You can begin a new game and start playing again.

When liquidating, be sure that all clients are notified of the situation. Unless there is an agreement among all lawyers, communicate with those clients whom *you* expect to continue representing. Get a formal, written authorization from the client to take files with you from the sinking firm.

Change is never an easy process, but during slow economic times, the defensive strategies outlined above can uncover opportunities for firms or individual lawyers to stay in the game and breathe new life into their careers.

CHAPTER 14
Tricks of the Trade

The greatest problem of communication is the illusion that it has been accomplished.
George Bernard Shaw

Chapter Checklist **Marketing**
Managing Your Finances
Handling Clients
Organizing Your Office

Following are some additional tips, techniques, or strategies that you can implement to help the business of your practice. Browse through them and pick and choose the ones that are applicable to your situation. (If you have any tips that you would like to share with others, send them to me at the address in the Preface for inclusion in subsequent editions of this book.)

MARKETING

Coordinate *all* your marketing communications activities—advertising and public relations—so that they work together. If you are going to engage an outside agency or consultant to help you, try to deal with only one agency for everything, if possible. This will result in less wasted energy and wasted money.

Consider *all* points of contact in considering your image as a marketing tool. Your stationery, receptionist's phone manner, attire—everything—reflects upon you and your firm to potential and current clients. Be sure that all these disparate elements are consistently communicating the message you want them to. After the substantive work of advocating your client's interests, everything else is marketing.

In advertising, remember the Four Ps: persistence, persistence, persistence, persistence. Print advertising needs to run a minimum of five or six times to be effective. Give any advertising program a chance to work. Conversely, do not change an ad campaign until you *know* it is not working. Just because you are tired of it, does not mean that your potential clients are.

Hire a marketing pro. When it comes to advertising, public relations, promotional material design, or other specialized marketing tasks, consider hiring a marketing professional (either an agency or individual). These people have already spent years acquiring the expertise that you probably do not have. They also bring a fresh, outside viewpoint to your problem solving. If you want it done right, hire a pro.

How do you find an advertising or PR agency? Clip out or note ads or promotions that you like. Call the advertising sales departments at the media in which you saw them (newspapers, magazines, radio stations, etc.) and ask them to recommend the agencies that are doing the work you like.

If you are doing your own public relations, develop a relationship with the media. Meet the editors. Become an expert in your field and get in their Rolodex by offering yourself as a quotable source. Be accessible—if an editor who wants to quote you calls, talk to him or her.

Consider having a crisis management plan. If you could be involved in *any* controversial or high-profile matters involving your firm or your clients, be prepared *in advance* to handle them. Designate a spokesperson as your official representative who will be the *only* contact person for the media. He or she should be senior enough in the organization to have adequate knowledge of all activities and be able to communicate effectively. It is important to act immediately and honestly in any crisis situation that involves your firm or its clients.

A free public relations mention of you or your firm in a newspaper or magazine is worth *three times* the same exposure from paid advertising. If you have a limited budget, go for the free PR first.

What is the best way to compensate an advertising agency? They will ask for a minimum retainer to bill against if it is to be an ongoing relationship. If you are interested only in short-term projects, offer to pay them a specific fee per project. When advertising, make sure you (the client) get the 15 percent agency media discount. Even if you work with an ad agency, have them pass on this media commission/discount to you and pay them only for the work performed. Discuss this *before* any financial arrangements are finalized with an agency.

Seven steps to successful advertising:

1. Find the inherent drama within your offering.
2. Translate that inherent drama into a meaningful benefit.
3. State your benefits as believably as possible.
4. Get people's attention.
5. Motivate your audience to do something.
6. Be sure you are communicating clearly.
7. Measure your finished advertisement, letter, brochure, or commercial against your creative strategy.

Hire a cheerful, caring telephone operator or receptionist. Since most clients go to lawyers only when there is a problem, a client who picks up the telephone to call a lawyer for the first time is already experiencing stress. The lawyer whose office staff facilitates the reduction of that stress will have a better client relationship and will also experience an easier time collecting fees. Staff must be courteous, must be helpful, and must be sure that the needs of the client are communicated to the lawyer. As an aside, with a good staff in place, the telephone can be viewed as it should be: the most effective, least expensive marketing tool available to every business.

Hire a cheerful, caring, conscientious secretary. When the lawyer is unavailable, the secretary should talk to the client and explain that the lawyer is in court or otherwise unavailable at the moment but will contact the client. The secretary should obtain a convenient time for the client, when the lawyer will be available to return the call, and make an appointment for a future call. "Telephone tag" is then decreased and so is the stress level of the client. Alternatively, if the secretary can handle the problem, then so much the better.

Return all telephone calls, especially when client deadlines have not been met. Be realistic in setting time constraints and discuss these with clients in advance. Clients do not like to hear that their document or pleading will not be prepared for ten days. However, they want to know the truth. It is worse to say the document will be ready in three days, and three days later when it is not prepared, to have to start dodging the bullets (i.e., the telephone calls). If the receptionist is rude or unsympathetic or if you dodge the client's call, the stress level of the client rises substantially. It is a client in this emotional state that will cause you problems. This client will speak ill of you to his or her friends and associates rather than sing your praises.

MANAGING YOUR FINANCES

By the old rule of thumb, expenses-to-revenue percentage used to be 50 percent. In the 1990s, that ratio is closer to 70+ percent. For every $1 collected revenue, $0.70 goes to operate the office. Thus, there is less left over for the lawyer than previously. Your goal should be to lower your firm's expenses-to-revenue percentage.

Consider using *Quicken* for financial information gathering on the computer. *Quicken* is the best-selling computer program of its kind, and it will write your checks, keep track of your check register, and prepare reports. The latest version (6.0) will even develop future budgets based on past operating results. And more than one bank account can be operated from the same program. One of the advantages of *Quicken* is its simplicity: you can master enough of it to be able to write checks and prepare reports in ten to twenty minutes!

Increase the size of retainers to improve cash flow. Most clients come to a lawyer because of a specific recommendation by a friend or colleague. They are concerned about the cost of the legal services, but they are usually not so price-sensitive that a modest increase in the size of the retainer will chase them away. The larger the retainer, the larger can be the portion of the retainer that is nonrefundable. Thus, your immediate cash flow increases.

Increase your hourly rate, a small amount at a time, until you are at least at the "market" rate—the rate your peers in the local area are charging.

Consider flat-fee billing as opposed to hourly billing. In a flat-fee billing, the entire amount of the fee can be deposited into the general account upon receipt. (Verify that the rules of professional conduct in your jurisdiction concur with this.)

Most clients prefer to know the total amount of the fee so that they can budget payment accordingly. They say they favor a known amount, even if it is large, rather than being faced with staring into the "big hole." To the extent the lawyer can properly estimate the total cost of the task, both parties will be happier.

Project contingency-fee billings. Most cases are settled without trial. The status of your present cases is known, the likely time and amount of settlement can be estimated, and the flow of future work can be projected based on your previous experience.

"Age" your accounts receivable once a week. This is an important piece of information in the management of your practice. Do not ignore clients who do not pay in accordance with their agreement. Time passes quickly when you are busily engaged in practicing law, advocating clients' interests. You tend to forget that one client owes you money while you are working on other clients' matters. Forgetting or ignoring "old" clients results in forgetting or ignoring the accounts receivable. With weekly review, you will be able to pursue collection with the regular, weekly reminders that money is owed to you, and you will be able to thank a client you talk to who has recently sent in payment on account. Such courtesies go a long way toward maintaining good client relations.

If, based on the aging information, you are aware that a client is delinquent in the payment of fees, stop further work for that client. Go to the beach, spend more time with the family, expand your marketing efforts for new clients, but under no circumstances should you do any further work for the client. Before stopping work, however, be sure the client knows that you will do no further work until payment is made. If the matter involves litigation, make the appropriate motion before the court to be relieved. Not only will you most likely get paid, but you will also see a better attitude in your client toward your efforts on his or her behalf. The client will know that you are serious, that you

Chapter 14: Tricks of the Trade

protect your own interests, and, therefore, will do all in your power to protect the interests of your client.

Maintain a high average daily balance. Most banks today calculate the "average daily balance" in your bank account. This is one of the most significant bits of information with which a bank works in analyzing a loan request. Thus, you want to maintain as high a balance as possible. This can be done either by keeping a large sum of money in the bank or by keeping limited funds in the account for a longer period of time. You can keep funds in the account longer by depositing revenue immediately upon receipt and spreading the payment of bills throughout the month. Do not pay your bills all at one time; this will cause an exaggerated dip in your account balance rather than provide an even flow of funds.

Do not wait to deposit checks. The first rule of cash-flow management is, Do not accumulate checks for deposit until the end of the week! While the check is "cooling its heels" in your desk drawer, too many catastrophic events might occur. The client may, in the interim, become angry, for whatever reason, and stop payment on the check. The check may reach your client's bank at a time when the account is overdrawn; the check is then returned to you marked "insufficient funds" ("nsf"). The client may have been named as a defendant in a lawsuit for which attachment procedures are available, and the client's bank account may have been attached and "marked" for a sum that is large enough to cause the presentation of the check you are holding to be rejected. In each of these cases, and many others that you can imagine, had the check been deposited immediately upon receipt, it most probably would have cleared the client's bank account.

Reconcile your bank statements immediately upon receipt so that any bank mistakes can be corrected right away and any mistakes made by you will be known and corrected before any embarrassment with the bank or your payee results.

Be sure that *you* sign all checks. Do not delegate this authority. You must know the present status of your business at all times.

Do not commingle trust funds with general funds. Bar associations generally have taken the attitude that even $100 of personal funds in a client's trust account is commingling of the lawyer's and client's funds and, therefore, a violation of the Rules of Professional Conduct.

In some states, by agreement between the Bar and banks, a trust account can be maintained even with a zero balance, and charges normally assessed by the bank will be taken from the general account. In earlier days, a lawyer had to deposit an "extra" $100 into the client's trust account. These funds were used to open the client's trust account and then to be sure that the bank would not close the account or remove clients' funds when charging fees and costs related to the account rather than the individual client. Today, most banks no longer require a $100 deposit to open or maintain a trust account. Therefore, there is no reason to keep this "extra" money in a trust account. The bank can be instructed to pay bank charges from the lawyer's general account. And, the Bar frowns, to say the least, on overdrafts in a trust account. There is no excuse for an overdraft in a trust account. In California, all overdrafts in a trust account are reported by the banks, for example, to the State Bar of California and will likely result in an immediate investigation. Further, some state bars will make random audits of clients' trust accounts. (The American Bar Association—House of Delegates—approved Report 119 dealing with a model disciplinary rule on random audits. More states will soon adopt this procedure.) Lawyers must now be sure that their trust account records are in good order and available for immediate inspection.

Maintain separate payroll and general accounts (of course, keep a separate account for clients' trust deposits/withdrawals). Either use an outside service or place in the payroll account the full amount of gross payroll (includes employee portion of taxes) on the day payroll is due. The general account should be maintained with only those funds necessary to cover the checks that are presented to the bank that day for collection. The balance of the funds should be "swept," per agreement with the bank, into a money-market account. Banks will perform this service automatically after you establish the initial minimums and maximums. You can modify these instructions at any future date.

Consider an automatic bank sweep. Banks today provide for an "automatic sweep" on a daily basis. Establish a minimum amount of money to remain in your general account, such as $2,500. The exact sum depends on the amount of checks and deposits that pass through your bank account each month. Then, instruct the bank to segregate all funds in excess of this amount at the end of each day and "sweep," or transfer, those excess funds into a money-market (interest-bearing) account until needed. Likewise, the bank can be instructed to automatically transfer funds back into the general account from the money-market account in the event the balance goes below the established minimum amount. The better approach, however, is to request the bank to call you on any day during which the balance of your account goes below the minimum amount established by you. This latter approach, as contrasted with the automatic sweep into the money-market account, forces the one responsible for these activities to know rather than guess the status of the cash balances at every given moment.

Make bank deposits personally until you know the bank personnel. Get to know the manager of the branch, the operations personnel, and the loan committee. These are the people who can help you the most when you have a need at the bank. Only when you are on good terms with the bank personnel should you either bank by mail or allow someone else in your office to make deposits.

Chapter 14: Tricks of the Trade

Negotiate immediate access to deposits. Some banks place a hold on funds deposited with them until the funds have cleared through the banking system. This may be as long as seven days. However, you can negotiate with the bank so that you have immediate access to your deposited funds.

Use special electronic devices to monitor facsimile and photocopy machines if you choose to bill clients for these costs. Recapturing these costs, while not universally accepted, can add up to a large amount.

Use a frequent-copier card. Most public law libraries have photocopy machines available where you do research. Rather than bringing a large amount of nickels, dimes, and quarters with you, buy a card with a predetermined number of photocopies available to the purchaser of the card. This card can be renewed from time to time. It is also a good record of photocopies for billing purposes.

Charge for the time of paralegals and legal assistants. "Legal assistant" has been defined by the American Bar Association as "a person, qualified through education, training, or work experience, who is employed or retained by a lawyer, law office, governmental agency, or other entity in a capacity or function that involves the performance, under the ultimate direction and supervision of a lawyer, of specifically delegated substantive legal work, which work, for the most part, requires a sufficient knowledge of legal concepts that, absent such assistant, the lawyer would perform the task."

The charge is not for secretarial work, but for creative legal work such as meeting with clients, meeting with court personnel, deposition summaries, drafting pleadings, contracts, etc., investigations, and generally assuring that deadlines are set and met.

Do not lower your fees. Lawyers take more cases than appropriate when they are temporarily not busy or when a client tells a tale of woe. Under those circumstances, lawyers even lower their fees. Guard against this inclination. Begin to upgrade the matters you take into your office. You can do this by beginning to raise your fee; clients will not balk at a modest fee increase. Clients generally do not appreciate, even sometimes do not know, that you are lowering the fee.

Analyze the "availability of funds" schedule at your bank. Depending on your bank's policy, you may not be able to draw out cash against checks in your deposit for several days. This problem (which benefits the "float" of banks) was serious enough that Congress enacted regulatory provisions that require banks to make public and announce their "availability of funds" schedule. Determine the number of days your bank will restrict your use of the funds in your deposits. Banks will negotiate a lesser number of days for a valued customer. If you are a valued customer of the bank and can negotiate either immediate access to funds or a shorter "hold" period, this will enhance your earning power. Even if you do not use the funds now released by your negotiation with the bank (or, in rare cases, the bank's own very short "hold" period), these funds will be available for placement into an interest-earning account with the same bank.

Consider a discount for clients who pay promptly. A percentage discount (e.g., 2 percent 10 days, net 30 days) may feel less than professional. An alternative would be to lower your hourly rate by $10 to $25 for the next month's billings as a reward for the client who pays within thirty days of original billing. Some may suggest that the converse should also occur, i.e., impose a penalty for those that fail to pay within the 30-day period. This, however, may be cumbersome and almost certainly will generate ill-will. Rather, if a client does not pay in accordance with the agreement (the initial written retainer agreement), then the better choice may be to cease doing work for this client and seek other clients.

Negotiate for a lockbox with the bank. In earlier times, the maintenance of a lockbox frequently meant that the accounts receivable had been assigned to a "factor" or other accounts receivable financier. Today, however, this is not the prevailing perception since banks have been advertising and heavily marketing the availability of lockboxes as one of their premier services. The bank picks up the remittances several times a day, records them, and then sends details of the transactions to the bank customer within several days. Modern technology (computers, etc.) allows the bank customer to be made aware of the deposit on the same day or the day following the deposit. This saves the time of opening the mail and processing the deposit. If a lockbox is not cost-effective, be sure that remittances that are received are deposited with the bank on the same day—absolute rule!

Mail accounts payable bills on their due dates. Creditors usually accept payment as timely according to the postmark rather than time of arrival (credit-card companies are the exception).

Get the best possible credit terms from your suppliers, such as the office supplies distributor and the library provider. Negotiate for extended credit terms wherever possible.

Record time as you perform the service, not later. Both "time sheet discounting" and "sloppy time-charging practices" must be avoided. Waiting until the end of the morning or the end of the day almost guarantees that you will lose a minimum of one hour every day (multiplied by 225 average work days in a year = 225 hours × your hourly rate of $100 per hour = $22,500 lost revenue/year).

Collect disbursable costs from the client in advance of your having to expend payment. These costs can include:
- Filing fees
- Deposition costs
- Traveling costs
- Major photocopy or cable costs

Do not open a new client file without a client-lawyer engagement letter specifically identifying the costs anticipated and the client's agreement to pay such costs in advance of your independently engaging or providing the service.

Do not take contingency cases without first planning for the costs of the case and determining that the outlay of those costs is an acceptable investment for you.

In a tight economy, your first reaction is probably to cut expenses. While this may be appropriate, expenses tend to be static and fixed. Be sure you are not cutting the meat of your operation, which will prevent you from taking on a new client later.

Revenue increases provide the most dramatic impact in a tight economy. Start by collecting old accounts receivable. Then, go out and get new business, first from existing clients, then from new clients.

Negotiate a reduction in rent. While this expense may be "fixed" under normal conditions, rent becomes a "variable" expense during times of economic difficulty. In most communities, office space is plentiful and landlords are thrilled to maintain their occupancy level as high as possible. Landlords prefer to avoid litigation over broken leases wherever possible. Therefore, under the right circumstances, landlords will frequently grant rent concessions if you make a fair and reasonable proposal, taking into consideration all the factors, including: (a) fair market rental value of your premises as currently occupied, (b) fair market rental value of comparable premises, (c) the financial condition of the landlord and his or her ability to absorb a lower revenue flow, (d) your financial condition and the urgency of the need to reduce costs wherever possible, (e) the landlord's perception of your needs, and (f) the existing relationship between you and the landlord.

You may consider showing the landlord your business plan, demonstrating that expenses are being controlled in all areas, that he or she is not the only source being asked to contribute to your successful handling of tough times. If you are reluctant to show your complete business plan, you may want to give the landlord a modified or shortened version of your plan in order to persuade him or her as to your future viability (the plan, of course, would *not* disclose the names of clients).

The next time you renew your office lease, think about taking along your lawyer and brokers. Many companies are hiring outside brokers at renewal time to generate competition between landlords struggling with escalating vacancy rates and developers of new buildings.

Consider hiring a law or auditing firm that specializes in lease audits. These audits verify that the "escalations" or "pass-throughs" in a commercial lease are not excessive. Such an audit could save you a significant amount of money in rent.

Part II: Techniques for Survival and Growth

HANDLING CLIENTS

Send to clients copies of all documents received in the law office and all documents sent from the law office. "Paper" the client. Keep the client informed. In this way, the client will get a sense of your activity on behalf of the client.

Tell the client what has happened immediately after it has happened. If the client is told what to expect, what is happening as it is happening, and what actually occurred, the client will then understand the entire process of his or her case and will feel that he or she is a participant in the process, not an observer. The client will fully understand and appreciate the diligent effort put into the process by the lawyer.

Spread your clients. No more than 5 percent of total revenues should come from any one client. Otherwise, you are at that client's financial mercy when he or she wants something, or you will suffer more severe consequences if and when the client's business departs.

Know when to say no to a client. This has two nonfinancial aspects. First, say no to a prospective client when he or she has had two or more lawyers before you on the same matter. There is trouble, and it is usually with the client. Also, when your best advice is ignored by the client, usually without telling you in advance that your advice will not be followed, you have lost "client control" and the respect of the client; it is time to withdraw from the case. When you say no to a prospect or client, be sure you put it in writing.

ORGANIZING YOUR OFFICE

Create and use the following management reports:

- Cash flow status report (daily)
- Accounts receivable aging report (monthly, but updated weekly)
- Conflicts of interest report (daily, as new clients come to the office)
- Marketing plan (revise it, perhaps quarterly; review it no less than once per week)
- Billable hours/unbilled hours (monthly)

Acquire or switch over to *WordPerfect* (version 6.0 is the current release) for your primary computer word-processing program. *WordPerfect* is one of the most powerful word processors on the market and probably the best all-around legal computer software tool. Most law firms use it.

Create a policy manual for office procedures. These procedures—set in writing for everyone (including temporary or replacement secretaries) to know, to follow, and to be measured against—are an important tool. However, such a manual is difficult for a sole practitioner to create. It should be created as time goes on; it should contain your form documents such as "thank you" letters for referrals; retainer agreements; opening letters to clients; format of billing statements to clients; and similar letters and forms that you have standardized for your office. The forms are easy to pull together in one location, either on a computer or in a file.

If yours is a multilawyer firm, do not let the committee run the firm. Despite the fact that lawyers are control-oriented, one lawyer should be charged with the responsibility of running the firm. And that lawyer should not be held to the same standard for billable hours or production of business that the other lawyers in the firm are. If the managing lawyer is held to the same standard, the firm gives little value to the task of management and growth. With little value being placed on this task, it is unlikely that the firm can grow or prosper, except perhaps by accident and then only for a limited time.

Glossary

Definitions of common accounting, marketing, and financial terms.

Accounts payable (A/P): A record of noncollaterized, short-term debt. Shown on the balance sheet as a current liability (due in less than one year).

Accounts receivable (A/R): Money due from clients carried as "open book" accounts. Carried in the current assets section of the balance sheet.

Accrual: The recognition of an expense or revenue that has been incurred but has not yet been paid or received.

- Expense: incurred but not paid or recorded.
- Revenue: for services performed or values created for which billing is not yet due.

Acid test: A measure of a company's solvency. Taken from the practice of pouring acid on mineral specimens to determine the presence and amount of metal.

Acid test ratio: A method of judging a firm's ability to meet current debt quickly. Formula: total cash + receivables/current liabilities. One common standard ratio: 1:1.

Aging of accounts receivable: An inventory of accounts receivable classified by how old each debt is; a method of estimating uncollected billing losses by aging the accounts and then assigning a probability of collection to each classification.

Amortization: Periodic allocation of the cost of an intangible asset over its useful life.

Amortize: To expense certain large costs incurred for activities that take place over several accounting periods by prorating them in some rational manner over the accounting periods involved; to liquidate a debt over time by installment payments.

Asset-based financing: Financing a business by using its hard assets for collateral to acquire a loan of sufficient size with which to finance operations; widely used in leveraged buyouts (LBOs).

Asset lending: The loaning of money on the value of assets offered as security. The lender is protected from loss by the liquidation value of the assets.

Assets: Tangible and intangible goods of value shown on the balance sheet.

Glossary

Balance: The net amount in any ledger account.

Book value: Total assets of a firm less total liabilities; owner's equity.

Bottom line: The profit shown on the bottom line of the operating statement.

Break-even analysis: A means of determining the quantity that has to be sold at a given price so that the revenues will equal costs. The formula for break-even points in units is: total fixed costs/(unit price – unit variable cost).

Break-even point: The level of sales at which total revenue equals total costs incurred; the point at which the firm is meeting expenses with no profit and no loss. Formula: Total revenue – total costs.

Bridge loan: Short-term, temporary financing used until permanent financing can be secured.

Budgeting: Estimating and planning income (cash receipts) and expenditures for a given period of time for various activities of the firm.

Business plan: An outline or plan for the owners/management to follow to a stated objective and, in some cases, to convince would-be lenders and/or investors to lend money to or invest in the venture because of its positive future. For internal purposes, the business plan consists of three essential elements—goals, marketing plan, financial plan. For outside lenders or investors (lateral partners), a more complete presentation is required.

Capital: Funds spent for the purchase or expansion of facilities, investment in personnel, advertising, furniture, etc.; also means money, cash, or capital expenditure.

Capitalization: A company's debt and equity structure; total amount of the various securities issued by a company.

Cash conversion cycle: The length of time required for the money spent for assets to be converted into cash again through sales and the collection of receivables.

Cash cow: A product or service that sells very well and has a low cost. The name implies the relative ease with which cash is obtained—like milking a cow.

Cash discount: The amount that may be deducted from an invoice, with the consent of the seller, for payment within a stipulated time period.

Cash flow: The most important consideration of a business's survival. The measurement of the differences between the actual cash received by a firm and its actual cash expenditures. Only the flows of cash are measured. Noncash transactions such as depreciation, amortization, credit sales, and purchases on account are ignored.

Cash-flow projections: A forecast of the cash flows for a period of time in the future. Sometimes called a cash-flow budget or forecast.

Glossary

CEO: Chief executive officer.
CFO: Chief financial officer.
Check: A negotiable instrument signed by the payor directing a financial institution to pay a specified amount of money to a designated third-party payee.
COD: Cash on delivery.
Collateral: The assets(s) that is(are) offered as security for a loan.
Collateral note: A note secured by an asset.
Commercial bank: A state or nationally chartered bank that accepts demand deposits, grants business loans, and provides a variety of other financial services.
Compensating balance: A balance that must be kept on deposit in a bank in order to support a line of credit. The net effect is to increase interest costs.
COO: Chief operating officer.
CPA: Certified public accountant; accountant who meets standards established by state law.
Credit: A transaction in which payment is to be made a later date; the right side of an account ledger.
Creditors: Firms to which money is owed.
Current assets: Cash or property that can be converted to cash in a short period of time, usually accounts receivable, inventory, and short-term notes receivable.
Debit: An entry of debt in an account; the left side of an account ledger.
Debt capital: Funds or assets acquired by borrowing.
Debt service: The money (principal and interest) needed to pay the amount due on a loan.
Debt-to-equity ratio: The relationship of debt to owner's equity or net worth in a firm's capital structure. The higher the ratio, i.e., the more debt there is relative to equity, the greater the firm's leverage.
Depreciation: The periodic allocation of the cost of a tangible long-lived (more than one year) asset over its estimated useful life. (Land, having an unlimited useful life, is not subject to depreciation).
Discount: An amount that a seller allows a buyer to deduct from an invoice under stipulated conditions (cash discount, quantity discount, trade discounts, seasonal discounts, etc.).
Double-entry system: A system of recording business transactions requiring that each transaction have equal debit and credit totals, thereby maintaining a balance within the accounts taken as a whole.
Downsizing: The scaling down of the number of people employed by a firm.
Earnings projections: The amount of profit a business expects to receive from future sales, investment, or other income-producing operations within a given period.

Glossary

Eighty/twenty principle: A rule of thumb in which a firm may get 80 percent of its business from 20 percent of its clients while spending 80 percent of its effort to gain the remaining 20 percent of its business.

Equity capital: Funds invested in a business by its owner(s), usually in the start-up phase.

Financial statements: Periodic accounting reports of a firm's activities. Usually includes the balance sheet and income statement.

Fiscal year: Any consecutive twelve-month accounting period used by a firm (does not necessarily coincide with the calendar year of Jan. 1 to Dec. 31).

Fixed assets: Property with a relatively long life, such as land, buildings, and equipment.

Fixed cost: A cost that remains constant during a relevant period of time.

Four Ps: In marketing, the components of the marketing mix considered to influence the consumer's decision to buy: product, price, promotion, and place. Sometimes, the four Ps are deemed to be persistence, persistence, persistence, and persistence.

GAAP: "Generally accepted accounting principles" as promulgated by the American Institute of Certified Public Accountants in New York.

Going concern: A broad, generally accepted accounting principle that refers to an assumption that an enterprise is a continuing operation, having the resources to meet its obligations and commitments.

Gross margin: In manufacturing terms, net sales minus cost of goods sold, sometimes known as gross profit. In a law firm context, gross margin is revenues minus operating expenses (before lawyers' salaries or draws); equivalent to "profit."

Gross revenues: The total revenues for a given period—includes billings that may be written off later.

Income statement: A financial statement that shows the amount of income earned by a firm over a specific period of time (accounting period). All costs (expenses) are subtracted from gross revenues (sales) to determine net income, which outlines the profit and loss financial statement.

Industry profile: The history, participants, total sales volume, trends, growth potential, and other pertinent facts on a particular industry.

Leverage: The use of debt financing, as contrasted with financing with owners' capital or equity. The greater the leverage, the greater the debt owed.

Liability: A debt of the business; an amount owed or an obligation to perform a service to creditors or others; a claim against assets.

Glossary

Line of credit: Short-term financing usually granted by a bank up to a predetermined limit; debtor borrowing as needed up to the limit of credit without need to renegotiate the loan.

Liquidation: The process of converting assets into cash.

Liquidity: The relative amount of ease in converting assets to cash.

Long-term debt: Loans that are to be paid back over a period greater than one year.

Long-term liabilities: Debts of a firm that mature more than one year ahead, beyond the normal operating cycle, or are to be paid out of noncurrent assets.

Market-driven: An enterprise created to take advantage of or exploit a market opportunity; a business that is based on providing what the market or customer wants, not what the business person wants to sell.

Marketing plan: A written formulation for achieving the marketing goals and strategies of the firm, usually on an annual basis; one segment of a business plan.

Market positioning: The projection of a product as having a certain desired image that makes it appealing to a certain segment of the market for that type of product or service.

Maturity: The end of a loan repayment period.

Net income: The formula for determining net income is calculated by subtracting all expenses and taxes from total revenue.

Networking: The establishment of communication channels with important people in a variety of related fields to provide information and contacts that can be used to help the individual become successful. It is net*work*ing, not net*rest*ing.

Net worth: Determined on the balance sheet by subtracting liabilities from assets.

Operating expenses: Costs involved in a firm's operations throughout a period of time, including selling, administrative, and general overhead expenses.

Overhead: Operating costs not directly associated with the product or its marketing such as rent, administrative expenses, etc.

Owner's equity: The resources invested by the owner of a firm; assets – liabilities = owner's equity. Also called residual equity.

Principal: The original amount borrowed or financed; interest is paid on the principal. The face amount of a note. As principal is repaid, the declining balance is called the remaining principal balance.

Profit: What remains from revenues when all operating expenses (including taxes) have been paid. Pretax profit refers to this amount plus the taxes to be paid. In a law-firm context, it is equivalent to "gross margin." Usually, law firm profits do not remain but are distributed to the lawyers as salaries or draws.

Profit margin: A measure of profitability; the percentage of each dollar of revenue that is net income. Formula: net income/revenues.

Glossary

Pro forma: Indicates a projection into the future, as with financial statements.

Salary: Consistent compensation from period to period that is not directly related to the number of hours worked by an employee.

Service: An intangible function that benefits the consumer.

Win-win: To negotiate a deal where both parties involved in a transaction satisfy their goals and feel they have concluded a satisfactory deal.

APPENDIX A
Cash Flow Projection Forms

Cash Flow Projection Form—Collected Revenue

CASH FLOW STATEMENT	Jan	Feb	Mar	Apr	May	Jun	Jul	Aug	Sep	Oct	Nov	Dec	Total
Cash Retainers Collected for General Account (not Trust Account)													
Transfer of Funds from Trust Account per Client Instructions													
Contingency Fees Collected													
Collected Accounts Receivable													
Funds Collected from Sale of Assets													
Miscellaneous Collected Funds													
Total Funds Collected													
*New Equity Funds Collected													
*New Debt Funds Collected													

Note: A cash flow projection can include 18 months of information. Review and revise the projection on a monthly basis.
© 1993 Edward Poll

Cash Flow Projection Form—Paid Expenses

CASH FLOW STATEMENT	Jan	Feb	Mar	Apr	May	Jun	Jul	Aug	Sep	Oct	Nov	Dec	Total
Employee Salaries													
Employee Taxes													
Partners Draw—Shareholder Salaries													
Rent													
Insurance—Health													
Insurance—General													
Insurance—Errors & Omissions													
Marketing & P.R.													
Office Supplies													
Phone/Copy/Fax													
Professional Dues													
Education													
Library													
Professional Services													
Travel & Entertainment													
Loan Repayment													
Total Operations Expenditures													

Note: A cash flow projection can include 18 months of information. Review and revise the projection on a monthly basis.
© 1993 Edward Poll

Cash Flow Projection Form—Summary

CASH FLOW STATEMENT	Jan	Feb	Mar	Apr	May	Jun	Jul	Aug	Sep	Oct	Nov	Dec	Total
Beginning Cash Balance													
Plus: Increases—Collected Revenue													
Less: Decreases—Paid Expenses													
Ending Cash Balance													
Plus: Short-term Loans Required													
Cash Available													
Less: Equipment Purchases													
Balance of Cash													
Plus: Long-term Loans													
Free Cash Flow													
Less: Minimum Saving Act.													
Net Free Cash Flow													
Less: Extraordinary Use of Cash Flow													
Net Free Cash Flow Carryover													

Note: A cash flow projection can include 18 months of information. Review and revise the projection on a monthly basis.
© 1993 Edward Poll

APPENDIX B
Monthly Accounts Receivable Aging Analysis

Monthly Accounts Receivable Aging Analysis

Month of: _____

Name of client	0–30	31–60	61–90	91–120	121–150	More than 150
TOTAL						

Accounts Receivable Aging Schedule by Percentage by Quarter

Days Outstanding	1st Qtr. (Jan–Mar)	2nd Qtr. (Apr–Jun)	3rd Qtr. (Jul–Sep)	4th Qtr. (Oct–Dec)
0–30 days				
31–60 days				
61–90 days				
91–120 days				
121–150 days				
151+ days				
Total:	100%	100%	100%	100%

Accounts Receivable Aging Schedule by Percentage by Month

Days Outstanding	Jan	Feb	Mar	Apr	May	Jun	Jul	Aug	Sep	Oct	Nov	Dec
0–30 days												
31–60 days												
61–90 days												
91–120 days												
121–150 days												
151+ days												
Total:	100%	100%	100%	100%	100%	100%	100%	100%	100%	100%	100%	100%

APPENDIX C
Profit & Loss Statement

Profit and Loss Statement
1/1/92 Through 7/31/92

All Accounts

Category Description	1/1/92–7/31/92
INCOME/EXPENSE	
INCOME	
4000-FEE INCOME	704,081.99
4020-BANK CREDIT MEMO	1,819.82
9999-VOID CHECK	0.00
Income—Other	0.02
TOTAL INCOME	705,901.83
EXPENSES	
1500-FURNITURE & FIXTURES	1,584.00
5000-ADVERTISING	1,108.70
5010-ACCOUNTANT	800.00
5020-ATTORNEY SERVICE	1,481.22
5050-LAW LIBRARY EXPENSES	14,471.91
5060-CONTINUING EDUCATION	1,845.00
5070-CLIENT COSTS	33,611.74
5071-COURT REPORTER	2,525.70
5072-COURIER SERVICE	4,153.66
5080-DONATION—REGULAR	205.00
5090-DONATIONS—POLITICAL	3,600.00
5100-DUES & SUBSCRIPTIONS	6,443.00
5120-EMPLOYEE BENEFITS	976.50
5130-ENTERTAINMENT & GIFTS	900.99
5140-EQUIPMENT RENTAL	770.77
5141-EXP. REIMBURSEMENT	2,002.38
5150-FILING FEES & COURT COSTS	1,392.00
5160-INSURANCE	19,518.04
5170-INTEREST	500.00
5180-MESSENGERS	4,131.36
5190-OFFICE EXPENSE	19,575.42
5200-OUTSIDE LABOR	13,690.97
5210-PAYROLL TAXES	100,104.63
5220-PAYROLL SERVICE	683.32
5222-ADD.FED.TAX	650.00
5230-PARKING	9,125.00
5250-PROFESSIONAL FEES	4,705.00
5310-TAXES—OTHER	7,369.77
5320-TELEPHONE	8,482.68
5330-TRAVEL—TRANSPORATION	4,396.41
5350-POSTAGE AND PRINTING	2,645.23
5355-RENT	54,000.00
5360-REPAIRS	1,478.68
5390-OFFICE SALARIES	187,925.05
5400-OFFICER'S SALARIES	138,990.00
5450-BANK DEBIT MEMO	3,854.96
9998-UNKNOWN TRANSACTION	1,053.93
Expenses—Other	0.82
TOTAL EXPENSES	660,753.84
TOTAL INCOME/EXPENSE	45,147.99

APPENDIX D
Budget Recap Revenue and Expense Forms

Budget Recap: REVENUE

Use this form to summarize projected and actual revenues and the amount of difference between the two. Show at least two years to spot any trends or patterns.

Month	Description	199___	199___
JAN	Projected Actual Variance		
FEB	Projected Actual Variance		
MAR	Projected Actual Variance		
APR	Projected Actual Variance		
MAY	Projected Actual Variance		
JUN	Projected Actual Variance		
JUL	Projected Actual Variance		
AUG	Projected Actual Variance		
SEP	Projected Actual Variance		
OCT	Projected Actual Variance		
NOV	Projected Actual Variance		
DEC	Projected Actual Variance		
YEAR TOTAL	Projected Actual Variance		

Budget Recap: EXPENSE

Use this form to summarize projected and actual expenses and the amount of difference between the two.

YEAR: _____

Month	Description	Salaries	Taxes	Draws	Rent	Insurance	Marketing & P.R.	Office Supplies	Phone/ Copy/Fax	Professional Dues	Education	Library	Professional Serv.	Travel & Entertain.	Loan Repayment
JAN	Projected Actual Variance														
FEB	Projected Actual Variance														
MAR	Projected Actual Variance														
APR	Projected Actual Variance														
MAY	Projected Actual Variance														
JUN	Projected Actual Variance														
JUL	Projected Actual Variance														
AUG	Projected Actual Variance														
SEP	Projected Actual Variance														
OCT	Projected Actual Variance														
NOV	Projected Actual Variance														
DEC	Projected Actual Variance														
YEAR TOTAL	Projected Actual Variance														

APPENDIX E
General Ledger Information

9/2/92	\	General Ledger Information			
Monthly	Fees Billed	WIP Fees	Fees Non-Billable	Fee Write-Offs	Accounts Receivable
January	$68,285.50	$1,172.40	None	−$15,163.00	$277,574.55
February	$54,095.50	$88,661.00	None	−$3,509.23	$270,439.07
March	$88,534.00	$86,470.50	None	−$99.00	$243,212.47
April	$91,270.50	$77,277.00	None	$8,458.61	$214,823.40
May	$186,103.30	$39,993.00	None	−$43,245.38	$352,484.08
June	$139,983.36	$122,375.30	None	−$18,290.58	$300,192.42
July	$138,116.50	$119,571.00	None	−$5,599.14	$365,856.60
August	None	$61,840.50	None	None	None
September	None	None	None	None	None
October	None	None	None	None	None
November	None	None	None	None	None
December	None	$82.50	None	None	None
Totals:	$766,388.66	$597,443.20	None	−$77,447.72	n/a
Monthly	Costs Billed	WIP Costs	Cost Write-Offs	Interest Charged	Sales Tax Charged
January	$9,798.96	$241.75	−$1,565.79	None	None
February	$12,671.59	$10,670.33	−$1,371.50	None	None
March	$3,065.82	$3,817.88	None	None	None
April	$1,996.25	$1,997.12	None	$.05	None
May	$17,239.14	$3,933.47	−$937.77	None	None
June	$8,692.53	$5,958.60	−$1,661.04	None	None
July	$8,757.97	$7,091.53	None	None	None
August	None	$3,373.05	None	None	None
September	None	$69.24	None	None	None
October	None	None	None	None	None
November	None	None	None	None	None
December	None	None	None	None	None
Totals:	$62,222.26	$37,152.97	−$5,536.10	$.05	None
Monthly	Discounts Allowed	General Payments	Retainer Payments	Withdrawn from Trust	Deposited to Trust
January	$925.65	$118,011.80	None	None	None
February	$601.35	$68,420.49	None	None	None
March	$1,935.95	$116,791.47	None	None	None
April	$2,707.70	$127,406.73	None	None	None
May	$4,777.80	$31,276.08	None	None	None
June	$4,842.90	$182,753.05	None	None	None
July	$1,961.30	$77,866.15	None	$100.00	None
August	None	None	None	None	None
September	None	None	None	None	None
October	None	None	None	None	None
November	None	None	None	None	None
December	None	None	None	None	None
Totals:	$17,752.65	$722,525.77	None	$100.00	None

9/2/92 **Quarterly General Ledger Information**

Quarter	Fees Billed	WIP Fees	Fees Non-Billable	Fee Write-Offs	Accounts Receivable
First	$210,915.00	$176,303.90	None	−$18,771.23	$243,212.47
Second	$417,357.16	$239.645.30	None	−$53,077.35	$300,192.42
Third	$138,116.50	$181,411.50	None	−$5,599.14	$365,856.60
Fourth	None	$82.50	None	None	None
Totals:	$766,388.66	$597,443.20	None	−$77,447.72	n/a

Quarter	Costs Billed	WIP Costs	Cost Write-Offs	Interest Charged	Sales Tax Charged
First	$25,536.37	$14,729.96	−$2,937.29	None	None
Second	$27,927.92	$11,889.19	−$2,598.81	$.05	None
Third	$8,757.97	$10,533.82	None	None	None
Fourth	None	None	None	None	None
Totals:	$62,222.26	$37,152.97	−$5,536.10	$.05	None

Quarter	Discounts Allowed	General Payments	Retainer Payments	Withdrawn from Trust	Deposited to Trust
First	$3,462.95	$303,223.76	None	None	None
Second	$12,328.40	$341,435.86	None	None	None
Third	$1,961.30	$77,866.15	None	$100.00	None
Fourth	None	None	None	None	None
Totals:	$17,752.65	$722,525.77	None	$100.00	None

Accounts Receivable Aging—09/02/92

Current	$135,721.40
31–60 Days	$58,383.09
61–90 Days	$55,328.40
91–120 Days	$20,557.32
Over 120 Days	$95,866.39
Total Accounts Receivable:	$365,856.60

APPENDIX F
Payment Pattern Analysis

Payment Pattern Analysis (by Averages)

Month of billing	First month after bill	Second month after bill	Third month after bill	Fourth month after bill	Fifth month after bill	Sixth month after bill	More than six months after bill
(% for Jan.)							
Jan.	$	$	$	$	$	$	$
(% for Feb.)							
Feb.	$	$	$	$	$	$	$
(% for Mar.)							
Mar.	$	$	$	$	$	$	$
(% for Apr.)							
Apr.	$	$	$	$	$	$	$
(% for May)							
May	$	$	$	$	$	$	$
(% for June)							
Jun.	$	$	$	$	$	$	$
(% for July)							
Jul.	$	$	$	$	$	$	$
(% for Aug.)							
Aug.	$	$	$	$	$	$	$
(% for Sept.)							
Sep.	$	$	$	$	$	$	$
(% for Oct.)							
Oct.	$	$	$	$	$	$	$
(% for Nov.)							
Nov.	$	$	$	$	$	$	$
(% for Dec.)							
Dec.	$	$	$	$	$	$	$
TOTAL	$	$	$	$	$	$	$

Index

Note: A page number in boldface indicates that the term is defined on that page.

Abandonment, complaints and, 3
Accounting procedures
   aging analysis, 101–103
   cash flow planning, 58, 64
   liquidity determination methods, 100–103
   outsourced, 53
   turnover ratio and, 100–101
Accounts payable (A/P), 42, 115, 132, **137**
Accounts receivable (A/R), 43, 88, 128, **137**
   aging of, 7, 16, 43, 94, 104, 115, 128, 137
   Collected Revenue Cash Flow Form and, 46
   collection of, 4, 48, 93–94, 117, 133
   financier, 132
   growth, cash needs and, 108
   Law Firm Economic Survey form and, 19
   need for a loan, 109, 115
   "turnover ratio" and, 83, 100–101, 108
   working capital and, 107
Accounts receivable aging analysis chart, 34, 99, 101–104, 134, 148
Accounts Receivable Aging Schedule by Percentage, 114, 149
Accrual, **137**
Accrual method of accounting, 43, 48, 115, 137
Acid test ratio, **137**
Action plan, for initiating planning process, 17
Administration practices, Law Firm Goals Questionnaire and, 25
Administrative staff, 82
Administrator, of a law firm and planning, 14–15
Advance payment, cash retainers and, 45, 47
Advertising, 27, 29–30, 32, 35, 37, 56, 57, 125, 126
Advertising agencies, 34, 40, 57, 126
Agricultural law, revenue fluctuations and, 100
Alice's Adventures in Wonderland analogy, 8
American Bar Association (ABA), 29, 58, 109, 131
   Model Rules of Professional Conduct, 109
American Institute of Certified Public Accountants, 140
Amortization, **137**
Amortize, **137**
Announcements, as a marketing tool, 33
Annual budget, 114
Annual fiscal statements, 114
Antitrust, major cases, contingency cases and, 48
Antitrust laws, and fee schedules, 73
Asking-price concept, of billing rate, 74
Assessment of practice, in marketing plan formulation, 28
Asset base, 114
Asset-based financing, **137**

Asset lending, **137**
Assets, 43, 46, 49, 113, **137**
Associate lawyers, 17, 18, 39, 122
Automatic bank sweep, 130
"Availability of funds" schedules, 131
"Average days billings outstanding," 100

Bad debt, 72, 91, 92, 96
Balance, **138**
Balance sheet, information gathering and, 16, 43
Bank by mail, 130
Banker
   establishing relations with, 112
   selection of, 110–111
Banks and loans, 107–115
   character requirements, 113
   financial needs, 107–109
   information needed by bank to process loan, 115
   loan requirements, 113–114
   loans as source of extra cash, 109
   relationship between lawyer and banker, 112, 130
   selection of a banker, 110–111
   services for law firms, 111
   types of loans, 110
Bankruptcy practice, 28, 123
Bank statements
   clients' trust accounts, 16
   firm's general account, 16
Bar associations, 16, 72, 73, 129
   local, 29
   state, 3–4, 29, 47, 58
Bates decision, 37
Billing, 18–19, 48, 83–85, 86, 88, 108, 115, 134
   accuracy, 85
   complaints and, 39, 40
   cycle, 97–98, 101
   hourly, 12, 18, 57
   low-billing periods, 105
   new collected billings, 93
   noncollection of fees, 72, 93
   patterns of, 105
   rates, 74, 115
   records and information gathering, 16
   statement, 44, 83–86, 88, 94–95, 97–98
   turnover ratio formula and, 100–101
   volatile billings and aging analysis, 103
Billing process, 83–89
   appearance of billing statement, 84–85
   client response, 89
   clients and, 84
   responsibility for, 84

Index

Billing process, *continued*
   time of bill preparation, 85–88
   time of mailing, 88
Blended fees, use of non-lawyers and, 79
Blended hourly rate, 76
"Bonding," technical competence and, 6, 83–84
Bonus funds, 55, 73, 122
"Book" cash balance, 61
Bookkeeper, cash flow plan use and, 64
Book value, **138**
Bottom line, **138**
Boutique practice, 28, 123
Break-even analysis, **138**
Break-even point, **138**
Break-ups, of major national firms, 5
Bridge loan, **138**
Brief description format, 85, 87
Brochures, publishing of, 27, 30, 33, 35
Budgeting, **138**
Budget Recap
   Expenses forms, 64, 155
   Revenue forms, 64, 153–155
Business of law, 3–10
   basic structure of, 5–6
   need to plan, 8–10
Business plan, 117, 133, **138**; *see also* Planning process
   basic steps in planning, 12–14
   example of good and bad plan, 11
   need for, 8–10
   three elements of, 67
Business strategies, 125–135
   financial management techniques, 127–133
   marketing techniques, 125–127
   tips to handling clients, 133–134
   tips to organization of the office, 134–135
Business structure, of a law firm
   Law Firm Economic Survey form, 18
   partnership, 18
   professional corporation, 18
   sole proprietorship, 18

California State Bar, 3, 58, 129
Capacity, bank loan requirements and, 113
Capital, 113, 115, **138**
Capital expenditures, 52, 62, 122; *see also* Equipment purchase
Capitalization, **138**
"Capital turnover," 108
Capped fee, variation of fee structures, 74
Carrying costs, of a loan, 113
"Carryover," 63, 64
Case file, payment pattern analysis and, 103
Case law, "reasonableness" of a fee and, 74
Cash accounting, definition, 43
Cash-back-to-cash cycle, 43, 44
Cash conversion cycle, **138**
Cash cow, **138**
Cash discount, **138**
Cash expenditure levels, Personal/Professional Expense Hierarchy and, 55
Cash flow, **138**
   analysis, 44
   bank loan requirements and, 113
   budget, 42, 55
   cessation of, 7–8
   client's payment of bills and, 88, 89
   Collected Revenue Cash Flow Form, creation of, 45–50, 53
   forms, 143–146
   improvement in, 68, 127
   inflow, 45, 48
   introduction to, 42–45
   management, 129
   negative, 64
   outflow, 50, 52
   Paid Expenses Cash Flow Form, creation of, 50–59
   patterns of, 105
   plan, 40, 44, 64, 99
   projections, 46, 114, 117, **138**
   Summary Cash Flow Form, creation of, 59–64
   uneven, 77–78
Cash Flow Expense Form, 35
Cash-flow statement, 16, 19, 42–44, 45–65, 113
Cash flow status report, 134
Cash management, on-line financial network for, 111
Cash retainers, 46, 47
   advance payment for work, 45
   "nonrefundable retainer," 45, 47
Certificates of deposit, 111
Cessation of work, 128, 132
Check, **139**
Checkbook register, 16, 72
Checking account, interest from, 49
Clerical personnel, employee salaries and, 53
Client authorization, transfer of funds and, 47
Client base, 16, 32, 115
"Client control," 4, 134
Client-debtor, 98
Client-lawyer engagement letter, 132
"Client satisfaction curve," 98
Clients, 5, 7, 13, 23, 32
   annual service, 30
   "carrying" of, 101
   "difficult," 93–94
   education of, 97
   existing, 37, 68, 83
   goodwill in billing, 72, 89
   "hype," 97
   needs of, 4, 38–39
   "one-time," 30
   prospective, 16, 27, 28
   raising rates with, 81
   relations, 6, 27, 115
   stress level of, 127
   techniques in handling, 133–134
COD, debt collection payment plan, 96, **139**
Collateral, **139**
   bank loan requirements and, 113–114
Collateral note, **139**
Collected Revenue Cash Flow Form, 46, 61, 144
   creation of, 45–50, 53, 60
Collection of fees, 48, 91–98, 127, 128
   methods of increasing, 93–98
   process of, 93
   seasonal fluctuations, 105

Index

Commercial bank, **139**
Commercial paper, 111
Communication, 32–34, 85, 97, 123, 125
    between lawyers and staff, 68
    two-way communication process, 94–95
    with clients, 38, 39, 40, 83, 89
Compensating balance, **139**
Compensation, 7, 71, 73, 83, 96
Competition, 28, 96–97, 99, 112
    for fewer clients, 7, 32
    market pricing and, 71, 73, 75
Complaints, 3–4, 7, 24, 39
    handling of, 27, 39–40
Computers, 19, 109
    billing programs, 84, 85
    financial programs, 72, 124, 127
    standard spreadsheet program, 42
    Wordperfect, 134
Conflicts of interest report, 134
Consultants, outside management/marketing, 34, 35, 40, 58
Contingency agreements, determining hours billed, 72
Contingency-based law practice, 12, 21, 49
Contingency cases, 79, 115, 132
Contingency fees, 46, 48–49, 74, 78, 128
Contingency recovery, financial competence and, 6
Continuing Education of the Bar, 58
Continuing legal education (CLE), 58; *see also* Education
Contracts, revenue expectations and, 37, 99, 131
Conversion cycle of assets, 108
Corporate Counsel, 84
Corporate minutes, 37
Cost-containment programs, 115
Cost disbursements, 75
Cost-plus pricing, 71–73
Costs
    "big ticket," 118
    external, 75
    internal, 75
County law library, 52
Creative legal work, 131
Credit, 68, **139**
    arrangement of, 111
    business practices and, 91
    policy with clients, 91–98
    terms, 108–109, 132
Credit card, short-term loan, 61
Creditors, 117, **139**
Creditworthiness, 92
Crisis management plan, 126
Cross-selling services, 30, 33, 35
Current assets, **139**
Custody disputes, seasonality of, 100
Custody (trust) services, 111

Debit, **139**
Debt capacity ratios, 115
Debt capital, **139**
Debt collection, contingency cases and, 48
Debt service, **139**
Debt-to-equity ratio, 113, **139**
Delayed payment, value pricing and, 77

Delegation of duties, 76, 79, 80
"De-mergers," 5, 122–123
Depositions
    costs, 132
    transcripts, 75
    summaries, 131
Depreciation, **139**
"Dial-and-Smile" technique, 89, 94–96, 98
Discount, 74, **139**
Discovery, contingency cases and, 49
Disbursable costs, collection of, 132
Double-entry system, **139**
Downsizing, 53, 122, **139**
Draws
    of associate lawyers, 15, 44, 52–53, 71
    beginning cash balance and, 61
    gross margin and, 93, 108
    of partners, 5, 7, 51–55, 71, 110
Due diligence, 114
Dun & Bradstreet, 92

Earned fee, 47
Earnings projections, **139**
Economic slowdown, 4–8, 10, 13, 121–123, 132
    demerger, 121, 122–123
    downsizing, 121, 122
    liquidation, 121, 123
    strategies, 121
    temporary slowdown, 121–122
Education, continuing legal, 51–52
Efficiency, of firms representation, 76, 81
Eighty/twenty principle, 83, **140**
Elder law, 123
Elderly, services for, 28
Employees
    training, 118
    compensation, 19
    morale, 68
Entertainment expenses, 51, 59
Environmental law, 28, 123
Equipment purchase, 52, 60, 62, 118; *see also* Capital expenditures
    funding for, 107, 109, 110
Equity, 113–114
Equity capital, **140**
Errors and omissions (E&O) insurance, 56, 115, 118
Estate plans, 37
Ethics, 113
Executive director, 5, 18, 117–119
    job of, 117–118
    measuring benefits, 119
    as profit center, 118
Expenses, 41–43, 50
    accounts payable and, 42, 83
    confidentiality and, 15
    cuts in, 132
    static and fixed, 132–133
Expenses-to-revenue percentage, 127
Expert witness fees, 75
External costs, 75

Facilitator, in a planning meeting, 15
Family law, revenue fluctuations and, 100

165

Index

Family time, as a personal goal, 23
Fax copy, 51, 57, 75, 95, 130
Federal ID number, 92
Federal income taxes, 44
Fee agreement, general authorization and, 47
Fee-based law firm, 21, 49
Fee/compensation agreement, 96, 97
Fee payment, client authorization and, 47
Fees
   advance discussion of, 96
   collection of, 6, 127
   fixed/flat, 12
   increases to, 131
   "reasonableness," 74
   schedules, 73, 74
Filing fees, 75, 132
Financial data for use in business planning, 13, 18
Financial management techniques, 127–133
Financial needs, of a law firm, 107–109
Financial plan, creation of, 13, 14, 24, 41–65, 67
   cash flow introduction, 44–45
   Collected Revenue Cash Flow Form, creation of, 45–50
   definition of, 42
   key terms, 42–44
   Paid Expenses Cash Flow Form, creation of, 50–59
   Summary Cash Flow Form, creation of, 59–64
Financial statements, 16, 43, 115, **140**
Fire insurance, 56
Fiscal year, **140**
Fixed assets, **140**
Fixed costs, **140**
Fixed expenses, 54, 56
Fixed-fee agreements, determining billable hours, 72, 79
Fixed fee, 74, 76–77, 82, 128
Flat-fee billing. *See* Fixed fees
Forecasting, 42, 47
   determining accounts receivable liquidity, 103
   of revenues and expenses, 50, 67, 68, 99
Foreclosures, 28
"The Four Cs," 113
Four Ps, 125, **140**
Frequent-copier card, 130

GAAP, **140**
General account, 45–47, 111, 128, 129–130
General ledger, 101, 157–159
General practice, of law, 21
Geographical orientation, of law firm, 22
Goals, 13–14, 21–25, 45, 67, 73
   action plan for initiating, 25
   of law firm, 22–25, 27
   personal, 21–22
Going concern, **140**
Good faith, extension of credit and, 91
Goodwill, of client, 40, 72, 84
Gross billings, 18
Gross income, 76
Gross margin, 93, 108, **140**
Gross payroll, 130
Gross profits, 44, 115
Gross receipts, 15, 18

Gross revenues, **140**
Growth
   of law firm, 19, 53, 82
   of revenue pattern, 100
Growth potential, executive director and, 119
Growth rate, cash flow needs and, 103, 107, 108, 109

Hidden assets, 115
Historical information about law firm, 16, 41, 45, 52, 72
   qualitative information, 28
   quantitative information, 28–29
Home mortgages, 111
Hourly rates, 18–19, 72, 74, 82, 128
   alternative pricing method, 75–76
   billing process and, 83
   lowering for prompt payment, 131
   price sensitivity and, 81
   projecting revenue, 49

Image, of law firm, as a marketing tool, 22, 25, 29, 125
Income, definition of, 43–44
   maximizing, 91
Income statement, 16, 43, **140**
Independent consultants, 118
Independent contractors, 53
Industry profile, 92, **140**
Inefficiency, "written down" billing and clients, 84
Information, gathering of relevant, 13, 16–17
   concerning firm finances, 16
In-house quarterly statement, 114
Initial written retainer agreement, 132
Insurance
   business interruption, 56, 114
   disability, 114
   errors and omissions, 56, 115, 118
   as an expenditure, 44, 51, 52, 56
   health, 56, 118
   liability, 56
   life, 114
   personal property, 54
   umbrella, 54
Interest-earning deposit accounts, 111, 131
Interest rates, for outstanding balance owing on a bill, 92
Internal costs, 75
Internal Revenue Service report, 111
Investigations, 131
Investment account, attorney's, 111

Judgment renewals, 37
Judicial system, and reliability, 39

KISS (Keep It Short and Simple), 42

Law, as a professional service business, 4–5, 7, 44, 51–52, 67
Law firm economics, collection of bills and, 93
Law Firm Economic Survey form, 17, 18–19, 29
Law schools, marketing competence and, 6, 24
Law firm goals, setting of, 21, 22–25
Law Firm Goals Questionnaire, 23, 25
Lawyer-client relationship, collection of debt and, 95

Index

Lawyer-creditor, 98
"Lawyering"
   outsourced, 53
   technical competence and, 6
Lawyers and law firms, desirability as borrowing customers, 110–111, 113
Lawyer's team, 117
Lease audits, 133
Lease negotiations, 37
Ledger cards, billing records and, 16
Legal press, financial competence issues and, 6
Letterhead, as a marketing tool, 33
Letter of engagement, 84
Leverage, 4, **140**
Leveraged buyouts (LBOs), 137
Leverage ratios, 115
LEXIS/NEXIS, 92
Liability, 43, 114, **140**
Library, costs of, 51, 52, 58, 118
Life cycle of the firm, 121
Line of credit, 61, 110, 111, **141**
Liquidation, 123, **141**
Liquidity, 113, **141**
Liquidity ratios, 115
Litigation, 98, 128, 133
   risk of, 115
Loans, 51, 59, 109–115, 129
   bank requirements for, 113–114
   default of, 114
   information needed by bank, 114–115
   long-term, 60, 62–63
   relationship with banker, 110–112
   short-term required, 60, 61–62
   sources of, 109
   types of, 110
   unsecured, 114
Lockbox, 132
Long-term debt, **141**
Long-term liabilities, **141**

Mailing lists, 37
   brokers, 33
Mailings
   expense of, 56
   preparation of, 33, 34, 35
Mail-order catalog business, 37
Malpractice
   collection records and, 95
   counterclaims, 98
   cross-complaints, 98
Malpractice insurance, 56; *see also* Insurance, errors and omissions
Management committee, 18–19
Management information systems, 19
Management of a law practice, 4, 5, 19, 115, 117–119
   as a banking area of concern, 112
Management practices, 25
Manager, of a law firm and planning, 14, 44
Managing lawyer, 135
Managing partner, 18–19
Manual, of collection procedure, 94
Market positioning, **141**
Market pricing, 73–74

Marketing, 4, 6, 25, 51
   art of, 34
   as banking area of concern, 112
   building signage, 33
   communications, 32–34
   competence, 5, 6
   direct mail, 30, 33, 34, 35
   director, 30
   elements, 41
   executive director and, 118
   expense, 56–57
   fear of, 37
   gathering relevant information, 13, 16–17
   industry standards of expense, 52
   legal trends, 16
   strategies, 30, 32–34, 45, 67, 125–127
   tools, 83, 85
Marketing Action Plan, 34, 36, 37, 40
Marketing Activity Checklist, 34, 35, 40
Marketing objectives, establishment of, 29
Marketing plan, 134, **141**
   creation of, 13, 14
   definition of, 27
   preparation of, 117
   setting of, 24, 27–40
Marketing plan elements, 28–37, 40, 67
   communications, 32–33
   current situation, 28–29
   evaluation of success, 35–37
   objectives, 29
   requirements for reaching target, 34–35
   statistics, 13
   survey results, 13
   target customers or clients, 32
Marketing Situation Questionnaire, 29, 30, 40
Marketing Strategy Grid, 29, 31, 34, 36, 40
Marketplace, perception of
   extension of credit and, 91
   valuing services and pricing, 78, 81
Markups, the billing process and, 83
Martindale-Hubbell Legal Directory, 29
Media, public relations and, 32, 34, 126
Media commission/discount, 126
Medical experts, contingency cases and, 49
Meganational law firms, 4–5
Merging, 122
Messenger services, 75
Minimum fee guarantee, 79
"Miscellaneous collected funds," 49
Model Rules of Professional Conduct (ABA), 109, 129
Modern technology, 132; *see also* Computers
Money
   financial competence and, 6–7
   as personal goal, 23
Money-market accounts, 111, 130
Monograph, of collection procedure, 94
Monthly Accounts Receivable Aging Analysis, 147–149
Morale, among associates and staff, 7
Moral turpitude, payroll tax violation, 54
Multilawyer firms, 135

Narrative bill format, 85, 88
National Association of Credit Managers, 92

Index

National Enquirer, 22
Negative cash flow, 64
Net income, 44, **141**
Networking, 35, 111, **141**
Net worth, 18, **141**
New cases, revenue expectations and, 99
New clients, raising rates with, 81
New debt funds, collection of, 46, 50, 62
New equity funds
    collection of, 46, 50
    long-term loans, 62
New law practice, beginning funds and, 61
Newsletters, as a marketing tool, 27, 30, 33, 35
Non-lawyers, use of, 79–80
Nonpayment of bills, three reasons, 89
"Nonrefundable retainer," 45, 47, 128

Occupancy costs. *See* Rent
Of counsel, 17, 18, 76
Office control techniques, 134–135
Office expenses, contingency work and, 49
Office supplies, expense of, 51, 52, 57
One-secretary firm, 53
Opening capital account, 61
Opening letters to clients, 134
Operating costs, 71, 72, **141**
    gross margin and, 108
    non-lawyer percentage of expenses, 52
Operating funds, collection of, 46, 50
Options, 37
Outside brokers, 133
Outside consultant, 125
Outsourcing, 53
Overdrafts, 129
Overhead, 57, 75, 82, **141**
    in cost-plus pricing, 72, 73
    use in determining pricing, 71, 74
Overlap of cycles, 44
Owners, of the law firm and planning, 14–15
Owner's equity, **141**

Paid Expenses Cash Flow Form, 51, 61, 145
    creation of, 50–59
Paid expenses, Summary Cash Flow Forms and, 60
"Papering" the client, 133
Paralegals, 18, 39, 79–80, 117, 131
Partner control, 115
Partner's income, reduction of, 122
Partners
    lack of trust between, 7
    the planning process and, 14–15, 17, 18–19
Partnership format, 18, 114
"Pass-throughs," 54, 133
Pay-in policies, 115
Payment of bills, spreading of, 129
Payment of fees
    guarantee of, 88
    incentives for promptness, 131
    late payment, 91, 93
    nonpayment, 93, 128
    one-time payment, 79
    slow payment, 91, 105
    time of least resistance, 98

Payment pattern analysis (PPA), 99, 103–105, 161–162
Payment pattern analysis chart, **104**
Payment plan, collection of debt and, 96
Pay-out policies, 115
Payroll
    accounts, 130
    administration, 111
    as an operating expense, 18–19, 52
    taxes, 53–54
Penalty, failure to pay promptly, 131
Pension plan, administration of, 111
Percentage fees. *See* Contingency fees
Perception of value received, 81, 82, 85
Performance history, 41
Personal banking needs, 111
Personal financial planning, 41, 111, 114
Personal goals, setting of, 21–22, 23, 24
Personal Goals Questionnaire, 23, 24, 25
Personal injury cases, 34, 48
Personal/Professional Expense Hierarchy, 55
Personal satisfaction, goal of, 23
Personal savings, 55
Personnel
    hiring of, 108, 109, 118
    policies/procedures, 25
    size, as a law firm goal, 23
Photocopying, 51, 57, 130, 131
    internal costs of, 75
    major costs of, 132
Planning meetings, 15, 17, 23, 25, 29
Planning process, 11–20, 24
    acceptance of, 15–16
    basic planning steps, 12–14
    definition of, 11–12
    gathering relevant information, 16–17
    logistics of, 15
    strategies, 7
Pleadings, 131
Policy manual, creation of, 134
Poll's basic business planning steps, 12–14
Postage, internal costs and, 75
Practice, needs of, 55
Practice area trends, 7, 23, 28, 30
Practice development, 25
"Prebill," 88
Premium pricing, 78–79
Press mentions, public relations and, 32; *see also* Media
Price sensitivity, 80–82
Pricing of legal services, 6, 71–82; *see also* Billing rates
    alternative methods, 75–79, 81, 82
    blended hourly rate, 76
    contingent or percentage fee, 78
    cost disbursements as an element of pricing, 75
    cost-plus pricing, 71–73
    definition of, 83
    fixed or flat fee, 76–77
    hourly rate, 75–76
    market pricing, 73
    premium pricing, 78–79
    price sensitivity and raising rates, 80–82

Index

retainer, 79
use of non-lawyers, 79–80
value pricing, 77–78
Principal, 113, **141**
Prior criminal records, expungement of, 37
Pro bono cases, 73, 74, 89
Product benefits, 112
Product differentiation, 112
Production line efficiency, 81
Professional conduct, rules of, 45
Professional corporation, 18
Professional dues, 51, 52, 58
Professionalism, 37
Professional law corporation tax return, 16
Professional service business, law as, 4–5, 7, 44, 51–52, 67
Professional services, "outside" professionals, 51, 52, 58
Profit, 22, 23, 43–44, **141**
price sensitivity and, 71, 81
Profitability, 30
fixed-fees and, 77
Profit and loss statement (P&L), 43, 151–152
Profit center, executive director as, 118
Profit margin, 93, 108, **141**
Profits per partner, 115
Pro forma, **142**
Projected expenses, based on industry averages, 52
Promotional materials, as marketing tools, 33, 37, 73, 76, 125–126
Public law libraries, 130
Public relations, 40, 51–52, 56–57, 125–126
Public speaking, as a marketing plan, 27

Qualitative firm information, 28
Quantitative firm information, 28–29, 32
Quantitative problem-solving capabilities, 112
Quicken, 127
Quotable source, 126

Rates
raising of, 80–82
reasonableness of, 38
Reader's Digest, 22
"Realization rate," 72
Receptionists
employee salaries and, 53
as marketing tools, 126, 127
Reconstruction experts, contingency cases and, 49
Records, of collection efforts, 95
Recovery arrangement, contingency cases and, 49
Recovery value, contingency fees and, 78
References
bank (professional), 92
personal, 92
Referrals, 30, 33, 35, 111, 127
of clients, 80
sources of, 28
Regional firms, 4–5
Remittances, 98, 132
Rent
concessions, 133
contingency work and, 49
as expenditure, 44
as fixed expense, 54–56
industry standards of expense, 52
Paid Expenses Cash Flow Form, 51, 52
Rental lease, 54
Reports, as marketing and financial data in planning, 13
Reserve policies, 115
Resources, and implementing marketing plan, 40
Retainer agreements, 134
Retainers, 45, 46, 47, 79, 81
advance, initial, 44
advance, monthly, 57
advertising agency and, 126
as collection procedure, 96–97
increase in size of, 127, 128
monthly, 57
revenue expectations and, 99
Retirement, as a personal goal, 23, 24
Retirement funds, Summary Cash Flow Forms and, 63
Revenue, methods of determining, 99–105, 108, 133
aging analysis, 100–103
payment pattern analysis, 103–105
revenue pattern analysis, 99–100
turnover ratio, 100–101
Revenue center, lawyer as, 118
Revenue flow, fluctuations, 100
Revenue pattern analysis, 99–100
Revenue per lawyer, 115
Revenues
collection of accounts receivable and, 48
contingency-based lawyers and, 49
definition of, 44
financial history of firm, 41
as law firm goal, 23
as marketing objective, 29
objectives of, 29
projection of, 42
quantitative law firm information, 29
temporary shortages of funds, 55, 61–62
vs. expenses, 50
Revolving bank loan, short-term, 61
Revolving line of credit, as bank loan, 110
Risk
of bad debt, 96
of bankers in loan repayment, 113
of nonpayment, 76, 78
Risk/reward sharing, 74
Rolling twelve-month cash flow budget, 44
"Rule of 72," 55
"Rule of Three," 71

Salaries, 15, 18–19, 44, 49, **142**
beginning cash balance and, 61
employee, 51, 52, 53
gross margin and, 93, 108
of lawyers, 44
shareholder's, 51, 52, 53, 54
Sales pattern, seasonal, 103
Sample accounts receivable aging schedule by percentage (chart), 103

Index

Savings, law firm
   for personal use or emergencies, 63
   for "valleys" in practice, 63
Schedule C, firm tax return, 16
Schedules of liabilities, 115
Secretary, 18, 117
   the communication process and, 39
   employee salaries and, 53
   outsourced work, 53
Seed money, 107
Seminars, as a marketing plan, 27, 30, 33, 35
Service, 6, 39, **142**
Shareholders, 17–19, 51–54
Short-term investment, 111
Simple statement bill, 85, 86
"Sleaze" factor, 37
Small firms, 14, 15, 55
   executive directors and, 117, 118
   operating costs of, 72
   ratio of personnel to lawyers, 53
   temporary slowdowns, 121
Solo practitioners, 18, 23, 55
   as a business planner, 14
   cost-plus pricing and, 72
   executive director and, 117, 118, 119
   operating expenses and, 52
   policy manual and, 134
   ratio of personnel to lawyers, 53
   temporary slowdown, 121
Specialty practice, use of market-oriented pricing, 73
Spreadsheet computer programs, 42
Staff, 19, 29
   administrative, 18
   banking services for, 111
   funds to supplement, 107
   industry standards of expense, 52
   involvement in business planning, 14
   layoffs of, 122
   postponement of raises, 122
   salaries as an expense, 51–53
Standards of effort, 72
Start-up capital, 107
Statement of cash, 42
Stationery, as reflection of image, 125
Substantive law, technical competence and, 6
Sue for fees, 95, 98
Summary Cash Flow Form, 50, 52, 59, 60, 146
   creation of, 59–64
Supreme Court, 73
Survival techniques, 69–136

Taxes, employee payroll, 51, 53–54
   failure to pay, 53–54
Tax returns
   determination of operating costs, 72
   information gathering and, 16
   of law firms, 16, 114
   personal, 114
   Schedule C, 16
Technical competence, 5, 6
Telephone expenses, 51, 52, 53, 57, 75
"Telephone tag," 96, 127
Term loans, 110
The Three Competencies
   financial, 5, 6–7
   marketing, 5, 6
   technical, 5, 6
Time and motion studies, 81
Time records, use in billing, 72, 75, 81, 84, 85, 86, 132
Transactional work, 12
Traveling expenses, 51, 52, 59, 132
Trends, aging analysis and, 102–103
Trust account, clients', 111
   cash retainers and, 45, 46, 47, 48
   debt collections and, 96–97
   deposits/withdrawals, 130
   information gathering and, 16
   overdrafts of, 129
Trust and estate services, 111
TRW, credit-rating services, 92
Turnover rate, 7, 99, 100–101, 115

U.S. Congress, 131
U.S. government agency repurchase agreements, 111

Value pricing, 77–78, 79
"Variable" expenses, 54, 133
Vendor terms, 107
Visitation disputes, seasonality of, 100

Western law offices, occupancy costs and, 56
Wills, 37
Win-win, **142**
Witnesses, contingency cases and, 49
WordPerfect, 42, 134
Workers' compensation, contingency cases and, 48
Workers' compensation insurance, 54
Working capital, 107
Working capital loans, 113
Working cash balance, 61
"Write-off" policies, 4, 72, 115

Yellow Pages, 32, 34